AND OTHER

MARCIA L. TATE

CORWIN PRESS
Classroom

For information:

Corwin Press
A SAGE Publications Company
2455 Teller Road
Thousand Oaks, California 91320
CorwinPress.com

SAGE Publications, Ltd.
1 Oliver's Yard
55 City Road
London EC1Y 1SP
United Kingdom

SAGE Publications India Pvt. Ltd.
B 1/I 1 Mohan Cooperative
Industrial Area
Mathura Road, New Delhi
India 110 044

SAGE Publications Asia-Pacific Pvt. Ltd.
33 Pekin Street #02-01
Far East Square
Singapore 048763

ISBN 978-1-4129-5224-8

This book is printed on acid-free paper.

08 09 10 11 12 10 9 8 7 6 5 4 3 2 1

Executive Editor: Kathleen Hex
Managing Developmental Editor: Christine Hood
Editorial Assistant: Anne O'Dell
Developmental Writer: Susan Hodges
Developmental Editor: Carolea Williams
Proofreader: Bette Darwin
Art Director: Anthony D. Paular
Cover Designer: Monique Hahn
Interior Production Artist: Scott Van Atta
Illustrator: Dana Regan
Design Consultant: PUMPKiN PIE Design

TABLE OF CONTENTS

Connections to Standards

This chart shows the national academic standards that are covered on each page.

MATHEMATICS	Standards are covered on pages
Numbers and Operations 1	11, 12, 19, 28
Algebra 2	17
Geometry 1	15
Measurement 1	9, 27
Measurement 2	9, 23
Data Analysis and Probability 1	21
Data Analysis and Probability 2	21
Data Analysis and Probability 3	21
Reasoning and Proof 2	23
Communication 3	13, 21
Representation 1	13, 25
Representation 3	25

SCIENCE	Standards are covered on pages
Science as Inquiry 1	29, 33
Physical Science 1	29
Physical Science 3	39
Life Science 1	33, 37
Earth and Space Science 1	35, 41
Earth and Space Science 2	41
Earth and Space Science 3	31, 43
Science and Technology 1	33
Science in Personal and Social Perspectives 4	31, 43

SOCIAL STUDIES	Standards are covered on pages
Social Studies 2	44, 50
Social Studies 3	46, 48, 56, 58, 61
Social Studies 4	44
Social Studies 6	54
Social Studies 7	59, 61
Social Studies 8	52
Social Studies 10	54

LANGUAGE ARTS	Standards are covered on pages
Language Arts 1	65
Language Arts 3	63, 67, 69
Language Arts 4	75
Language Arts 5	73, 80
Language Arts 6	71, 79
Language Arts 8	77

Introduction

An ancient Chinese proverb claims: "Tell me, I forget. Show me, I remember. Involve me, I understand." This timeless saying insinuates what all educators should know: Unless students are involved and actively engaged in learning, true learning rarely occurs.

The latest brain research reveals that both the right and left hemispheres of the brain should be engaged in the learning process. This is important because the hemispheres talk to one another over the corpus callosum, the structure that connects them. No strategies are better designed for this purpose than graphic organizers and visuals. Both of these strategies engage students' visual modality. More information goes into the brain visually than through any other modality. Therefore, it makes sense to take advantage of students' visual strengths to reinforce and make sense of learning.

How to Use This Book

The activities in this book cover the content areas and are designed using strategies that actively engage the brain. They are presented in the way the brain learns best, to make sure students get the most out of each lesson: focus activity, modeling guided practice, check for understanding, independent practice, and closing. Go through each step to ensure that students will be fully engaged in the concept being taught and understand its purpose and meaning.

Each step-by-step activity provides one or more visual tools students can use to make important connections between related concepts, structure their thinking, organize ideas logically, and reinforce learning. Graphic organizers and visuals include: word web, KNL chart, Venn diagram, sequence chart, bar graph, T-chart, hand signals, floor graph, concrete model, cause-and-effect chart, bulletin board display, pattern mat, mind map, word wall, pictures, word cards, and more!

These brain-compatible activities are sure to engage and motivate every student's brain in your classroom! Watch your students change from passive to active learners as they process visual concepts into learning that is not only fun, but also remembered for a lifetime.

Put It Into Practice

L
ecture and repetitive worksheets have long been the traditional way of delivering knowledge and reinforcing learning. While some higher-achieving students may engage in this type of learning, educators now know that actively engaging students' brains is not a luxury, but a necessity if students are truly to acquire and retain content, not only for tests, but for life.

The 1990s were dubbed the Decade of the Brain, because millions of dollars were spent on brain research. Educators today should know more about how students learn than ever before. Learning style theories that call for student engagement have been proposed for decades, as evidenced by research such as Howard Gardner's theory of multiple intelligences (1983), Bernice McCarthy's 4MAT Model (1990), and VAKT (visual, auditory, kinesthetic, tactile) learning styles theories.

I have identified 20 strategies that, according to brain research and learning style theory, appear to correlate with the way the brain learns best. I have observed hundreds of teachers—regular education, special education, and gifted. Regardless of the classification or grade level of the students, exemplary teachers consistently use these 20 strategies to deliver memorable classroom instruction and help their students understand and retain vast amounts of content.

These 20 brain-based instructional strategies include the following:

1. Brainstorming and Discussion

2. Drawing and Artwork

3. Field Trips

4. Games

5. Graphic Organizers, Semantic Maps, and Word Webs

6. Humor

7. Manipulatives, Experiments, Labs, and Models

8. Metaphors, Analogies, and Similes

9. Mnemonic Devices

10. Movement

11. Music, Rhythm, Rhyme, and Rap

12. Project-based and Problem-based Instruction

13. Reciprocal Teaching and Cooperative Learning

14. Role Plays, Drama, Pantomimes, Charades

15. Storytelling

16. Technology

17. Visualization and Guided Imagery

18. Visuals

19. Work Study and Apprenticeships

20. Writing and Journals

This book features Strategy 5: Graphic Organizers, Semantic Maps, and Word Webs, and Strategy 18: Visuals. Both of these strategies focus on integrating the visual and verbal elements of learning. Picture thinking, visual thinking, and visual/spatial learning is the phenomenon of thinking through visual processing. Since 90% of the brain's sensory input comes from visual sources, it stands to reason that the most powerful influence on learners' behavior is concrete, visual images. (Jensen, 1994) In addition, linking verbal and visual images increases students' ability to store and retrieve information. (Ogle, 2000)

Graphic organizers are visual representations of linear ideas that benefit both left and right hemispheres of the brain. They assist us in making sense of information, enable us to search for patterns, and provide an organized tool for making important conceptual connections. Graphic organizers, also known as word webs or semantic, mind, and concept maps, can be used to plan lessons or present information to students. Once familiar with the technique, students should be able to construct their own graphic organizers, reflecting their understanding of the concepts taught.

Because we live in a highly visual world, using visuals as a teaching strategy makes sense. Each day, students are overwhelmed with images from video games, computers, and television. Visual strategies capitalize specifically on the one modality that many students use consistently and have developed extensively—the visual modality. Types of visuals include overheads, maps, graphs, charts, and other concrete objects and artifacts that clarify learning. Since so much sensory input comes from visual sources, pictures, words, and learning-related artifacts around the classroom take on exaggerated importance in students' brains. Visuals such as these provide learning support and constant reinforcement.

These memorable strategies help students make sense of learning by focusing on the ways the brain learns best. Fully supported by the latest brain research, these strategies provide the tools you need to boost motivation, energy, and most important, the academic achievement of your students.

CHAPTER 1

Mathematics

More or Less: T-Chart

Skills Objective

Use measuring instruments or nonstandard measurement tools to compare objects.

Materials

More or Less reproducible

balance scale

small objects (softball, ruler, block, pennies, book)

A **T-Chart** is a useful tool for making comparisons between two objects. In the following activity, students use a T-chart to record the relative weights of classroom objects.

1. Display two objects, such as a softball and a ruler. Ask students: *How could I figure out which object weighs more?* Students might suggest guessing, picking up the two objects to compare them, or using a balance scale.

2. Demonstrate how to use a balance scale to compare the weight of the two objects. Point out that the item that is lower on the scale is the heavier item.

3. Ask students: *How can I remember which item was heavier?* Lead students to understand that writing the information will help them remember it. Make a T-chart on the board with the column headings *More* and *Less.* Draw the item that weighs more (*softball*) in the first column and the item that weighs less (*ruler*) in the second column.

4. Place the balance scale in the science center along with objects students can weigh, such as blocks, pennies, and books.

5. Give students a copy of the **More or Less reproducible (page 10)**. Invite them to work in pairs to weigh the objects, and then record their results on the T-chart.

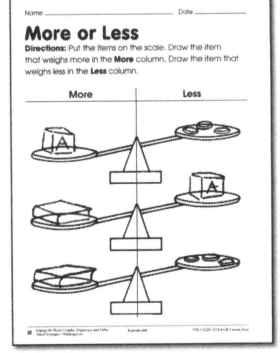

More or Less

Directions: Put the items on the scale. Draw the item that weighs more in the **More** column. Draw the item that weighs less in the **Less** column.

More	Less

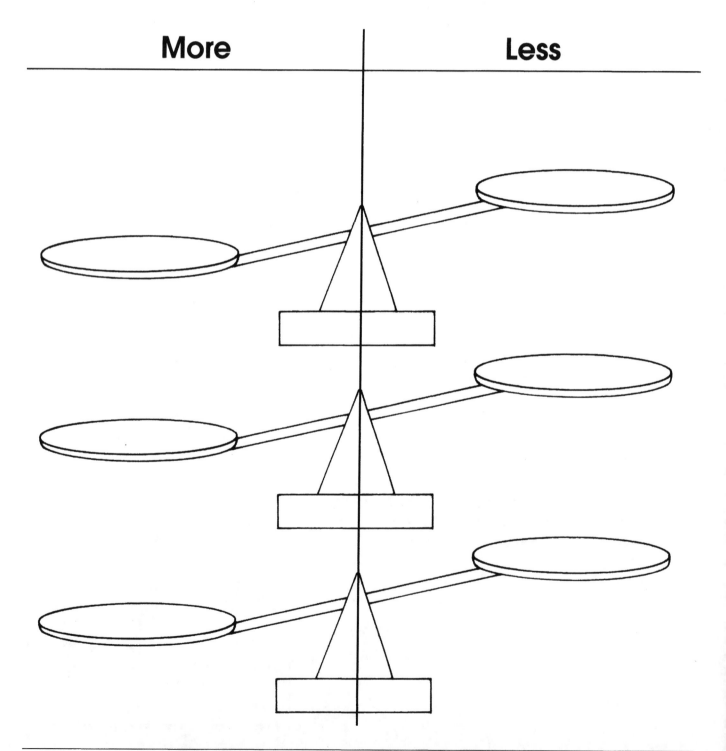

 Engage the Brain: Graphic Organizers and Other Visual Strategies • Kindergarten   *Reproducible*   978-1-4129-5224-8 • © Corwin Press

Number Race: Bar Graph

Skills Objectives
Count and recognize how many objects are in a set.
Graphically represent mathematical data.

Materials
Number Race
Results reproducible

dice

overhead projector

crayons or markers

Bar Graphs are one of the simplest ways to visually represent data. In this activity, students roll a die, count the dots, and record the number on a chart. As they repeat this process, they create a bar graph.

1. Show students a die. Have them count the dots on each side. Establish that each of the six sides has a different number of dots, from 1 to 6.

2. Demonstrate how to roll the die, count the dots, and say and write the corresponding number.

3. Repeat Step 2 several times. Explain that you want to find out which number is rolled most often. Suggest holding a number race to see which number is the "winner."

4. Make a transparency of the **Number Race Results reproducible (page 12)**. Demonstrate how to roll the die, write the number in the correct column on the bar graph, and then color the box. Ask volunteers to roll the die, write the number, and color the corresponding box.

5. Give students a copy of the Number Race Results reproducible and a die. Invite students to roll the die ten times and fill in a square in the corresponding number column each time. Suggest that students use a different color for each number.

6. Discuss and interpret the results of the number race with students. Ask them to identify the number rolled most often and the number rolled least often.

Extended Learning
- Have students conduct number races for several days and compare each day's results. Does the same number "win" each day?

- Cover the dots at the bottom of the Number Race Results reproducible. Observe students as they roll a number and write the corresponding numeral to informally assess their knowledge of numerals.

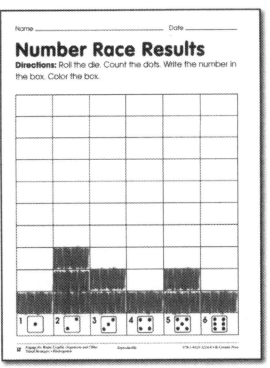

Number Race Results

Directions: Roll the die. Count the dots. Write the number in the box. Color the box.

1	2	3	4	5	6

Picture the Problem: Drawing

Skills Objective
Draw pictures to represent mathematical problems.

Materials
Picture the Problem reproducible

crayons or markers

Drawing is a useful strategy for developing number sense. By creating pictures, students can graphically represent their understanding of mathematical concepts. In this activity, students draw pictures that demonstrate their understanding of numbers and patterns.

1. Write a sentence such as the following on the board: *May had six shirts. Some were plain and some had stripes.*

2. Read the problem aloud. Tell students that one way to better understand this problem is to draw a picture. You will reread the sentence for clues about what to draw. Think aloud as you point out the clue six shirts, and draw six shirts on the board. Reread the sentence, *Some were plain and some had stripes.* Explain that this means at least one shirt was plain and at least one had stripes. Add stripes to one shirt and leave one plain. Add stripes to as many others as you wish.

3. Ask students to suggest other ways of representing this sentence, such as two plain shirts and four striped, or three plain shirts and three striped. Invite volunteers to draw their suggestions on the board.

4. Give students a copy of the **Picture the Problem reproducible (page 14).** Write another problem on the board. Have students use the graphic organizer to draw pictures that represent the problem.

5. Invite students to compare their drawings in small groups and discuss the different ways in which they represented the information.

Extended Learning
- Have students draw pictures to represent simple addition and subtraction problems.

- Invite students to draw pictures and then write or dictate number stories that interpret their drawings.

Picture the Problem

Directions: Draw a picture to show the math problem.

Shouting for Shapes: Venn Diagram

Skills Objective
Sort shapes according to attributes.

A **Venn Diagram** is a concrete sorting tool that allows students to visualize similarities and differences. Sorting items according to attributes is an essential skill for young learners. In this activity, students sort geometric shapes according to attributes such as shape and color.

1. Place two plastic hoops side by side on the floor, and ask students to watch as you place a paper triangle in one hoop and two paper squares in the other. Think aloud and explain what you are doing using the words *triangle* and *square*.

2. Have students suggest a label for each circle. With their help, use sticky notes to label the two hoops.

3. Have volunteers continue sorting the remaining shapes. Ask them to think aloud and explain why they placed each shape in a particular hoop.

4. Show students the house shape and ask them to determine in which hoop it belongs. Establish that this shape is both a square and a triangle. Ask them to brainstorm solutions.

5. Overlap the two hoops to form a Venn diagram. Demonstrate how the house shape fits into the middle section. Ask students to suggest a label for this section.

6. Give students a copy of the **Shouting for Shapes reproducible (page 16)** and a set of paper shapes (triangles, squares, house). Invite students to think aloud as they sort the shapes. Circulate among students to check for understanding and offer assistance as needed.

7. Have students glue the sorted shapes in place on their Venn diagrams and write a label below each section.

Extended Learning
Provide copies of the Shouting for Shapes reproducible and shape manipulatives in a learning center for independent practice.

Materials
Shouting for Shapes reproducible

large plastic hoops

paper shapes (triangles and squares)

house shape (square with triangle roof)

sticky notes

glue

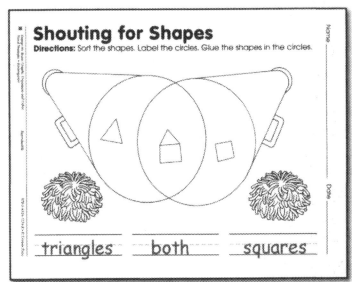

Shouting for Shapes

Directions: Sort the shapes. Label the circles. Glue the shapes in the circles.

Here Comes the Pattern Train: Pattern Mat

Skills Objective
Identify and create ABAB patterns.

Recognizing and creating patterns helps students make sense of mathematics. In this activity, students use a **Pattern Mat** to create an ABAB pattern with manipulatives.

1. Invite four students to stand in front of the class in an ABAB pattern (boy, girl, boy, girl). Ask the class to identify the pattern. Explain that this is an ABAB pattern. Give each student in the "pattern" an A or B letter card to hold in front of them.

2. Explore other ways of creating ABAB patterns with students. They might choose to create patterns using shoe type or hair color. Use the A and B letter cards to label each pattern.

3. Make a transparency of the **Pattern Trains reproducible (page 18)**, and give students a photocopy. Demonstrate how to arrange the manipulatives in an ABAB color pattern. Model how to color the train cars on the pattern mat in the corresponding colors. Label the train *ABAB*.

4. Give students counters in various colors. Invite them to create ABAB patterns and then color and label their pattern trains. If students need assistance, begin a pattern and have them complete it.

5. Encourage students to share their pattern trains with the class and "read" each pattern (*red, blue, red, blue*) aloud.

Extended Learning
Once students have mastered ABAB patterns, have them use the Pattern Trains reproducible to create ABCABC and AABB patterns.

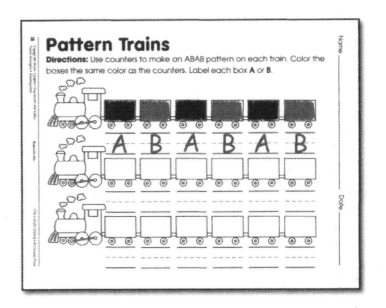

Pattern Trains

Directions: Use counters to make an ABAB pattern on each train. Color the boxes the same color as the counters. Label each box **A** or **B**.

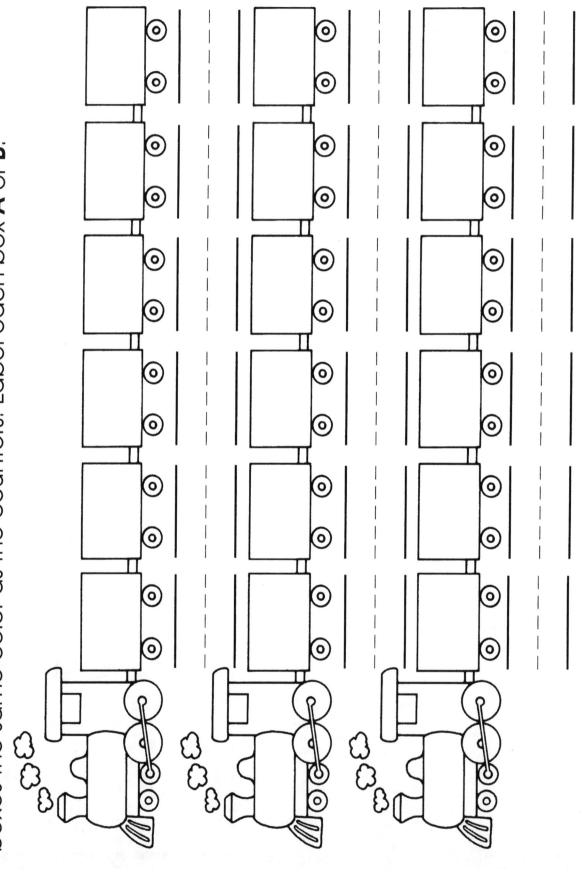

Engage the Brain: Graphic Organizers and Other Visual Strategies • Kindergarten   Reproducible   978-1-4129-5224-8 • © Corwin Press

My Monthly Calendar: Calendar

Skills Objective
Recognize, write, and name cardinal numbers to 31.

Calendar activities develop students' sense of time and reinforce counting and number recognition skills. The class calendar is an important part of the daily routine in many kindergarten classrooms. This activity gives students the opportunity to create their own calendar using a graphic organizer.

Materials
My Monthly Calendar reproducible

file folders

crayons or markers

1. Before reproducing the **My Monthly Calendar reproducible (page 20)**, fill in the name of the month and write the dates in the boxes. (Later in the year, leave the calendar blank before reproducing to allow children to fill in the boxes themselves.) Make a calendar folder for each student by stapling a calendar inside a file folder.

2. On the first day of the month, give each student a prepared calendar folder. Read the name of the month together. Help students locate the square for the first day of the month and trace (or write) the number in that square.

3. Each day, have students open their calendar folder, trace or write the number in that day's square, and color the square. On Mondays, have students fill in the dates from the previous weekend. Count the days together.

4. At the end of the month, students can take home their calendar folders to share with their families.

Name _____ Date _____

My Monthly Calendar

Month: _____

Year: _____

Sunday	Monday	Tuesday	Wednesday	Thursday	Friday	Saturday

Engage the Brain: Graphic Organizers and Other Visual Strategies • Kindergarten   *Reproducible*   978-1-4129-5224-8 • © Corwin Press

Me Tree: Glyph

Skills Objectives

Create a glyph that communicates personal information.
Read and interpret glyphs.

Materials
Me Tree reproducible

chart paper

crayons or markers

A **Glyph** is a method of representing data pictorially. Each symbol in a glyph communicates a different piece of information. In this activity, students create a tree glyph that provides personal information about them.

1. Draw an outline of a tree on chart paper. Give each student a copy of the **Me Tree reproducible (page 22)** and some crayons.

2. Explain to students that you are going to make a tree picture that shows information about you, and they will make a tree picture that shows information about them.

3. Ask students to listen closely as you read the following instructions. Model the activity using your tree outline. Pause to allow time for students to complete their own page. Check progress after each step.

   - *If you're a boy, color your tree trunk brown. If you're a girl, color your tree trunk red.*
   - *If you're five years old, draw five clouds in the sky. If you're six years old, draw six clouds in the sky.*
   - *If you like spring better than fall, color the leaves green. If fall is your favorite, color the leaves orange.*
   - *If you have brothers or sisters, color the sun yellow. If you do not have brothers or sisters, color the sun orange.*
   - *If you have a pet, color the bird blue. If you do not have a pet, color the bird pink.*

4. Display completed glyphs. Create a key to remind students what each symbol means. Discuss the results.

   - *How many students in our class are boys? How many are girls?*
   - *How many students have brothers or sisters?*
   - *If you want to know how many students have pets, how can you tell by looking at the glyphs?*
   - *How could you help someone learn to read a glyph?*

Me Tree

Directions: Listen to the directions from your teacher. Color the tree to tell about yourself.

Count a Handful: Picture Chart

Skills Objective
Estimate and count the number of items a student can grab in one hand.

A **Picture Chart** provides a visual representation of data. Prediction is one skill that students develop through repeated practice. In this activity, students predict how many items they can grab in one hand and then test their prediction by counting the items.

1. Display a tub of small items. Talk with students about what it means to grab a handful of something. Ask students to predict how many items from the tub they think you can grab in one handful.

2. Write their predictions on the board. Grab a handful of the items. Ask students: *How can we find out how many items I grabbed?* Count the items together.

3. Discuss the actual number of items and compare this number to students' predictions.

4. Give each student a **Count a Handful reproducible (page 24)** and a supply of small objects to count. Model the following steps:

   a. Predict how many items can be grabbed in a handful.
   b. Write and draw this number on the left hand of the reproducible.
   c. Grab a handful of items.
   d. Count the items.
   e. Write and draw this number on the right hand on the reproducible.

5. Have students discuss the results in small groups. Talk about why the numbers varied.

Extended Learning
- Repeat this activity with a variety of items. Ask students to explain why the number of items they can pick up changes.

- Once students are familiar with this activity, have them grab, count, and compare two handfuls.

Count a Handful

Directions: Predict how many items you can grab in one hand. Write and draw the number on **Hand 1**. Grab a handful. Count the items. Write and draw the number on **Hand 2**.

2. I can grab

1. I think I can grab

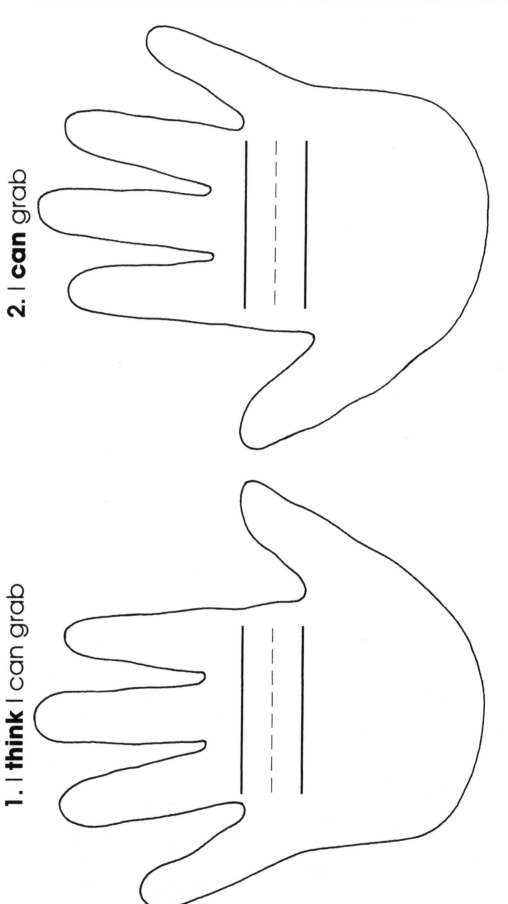

Laces or Not? Floor Graph

Skills Objective
Graph tangible items.

Floor Graphs enable students to graph using tangible objects and are ideal for first graphing activities. You can purchase a floor graph mat commercially or make your own from a shower curtain.

Materials
solid color vinyl shower curtain

black vinyl tape

permanent marker

plastic hoop

erasable pen or large sticky note

Making the Mat

1. Spread out a shower curtain on the floor. Use black vinyl tape or a permanent marker to draw a T-chart on one side of the shower curtain.

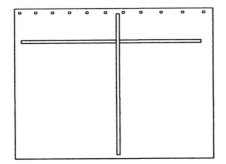

2. Turn over the shower curtain. Use a plastic hoop as a guide to draw two interlocking circles on this side.

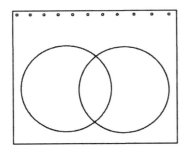

Using the Mat

1. Lead students in a discussion about their shoes. Talk about the different kinds of shoe fastenings. Then ask: *Do you think most of the shoes we are wearing have laces or don't have laces? How can we find out?* Guide students to conclude that they could use a graph.

2. Spread the graph mat on the floor. Using an erasable pen or a large sticky note, label the two columns *Laces* and *No Laces*.

3. Ask students to remove one shoe and place it in the appropriate column on the mat. Encourage students to think aloud as they sort and explain why they sorted their shoes as they did.

4. After all students have sorted their shoes, ask them: *Which column has more shoes? How can we tell?* Confirm the prediction by counting the shoes. Discuss how the graph helped students see the solution to the problem.

Extended Learning

Sort the shoes again using the Venn diagram side of the mat. Place shoes with laces in one circle, shoes with Velcro in the other circle, and shoes with both in the middle circle. Place shoes with neither laces nor Velcro outside the mat. Discuss the differences between this graph and the T-chart graph.

Measure This: Bar Graph

Skills Objective
Compare the length of classroom items.

A **Bar Graph** presents facts in a visual form that makes reading and comparing data easier. In this activity, students use lengths of yarn or ribbon to measure classroom objects, and then use the yarn or ribbon to create bars on a graph.

1. Draw students' attention to a classroom item, such as a table. Ask students: *How long do you think this table is? How can we find out?* Guide students to conclude that you can measure the table.

2. With the help of a volunteer, cut a piece of yarn or ribbon the length of the table. Write the word *table* on an index card, and tape it to the yarn or ribbon.

3. Invite students to work in pairs to measure different items in the classroom, using yarn or ribbon to show the length and labeling the items with index cards.

4. Help students sort the yarn lengths from shortest to longest, and arrange them on a bulletin board. Label the items to create a simple bar graph.

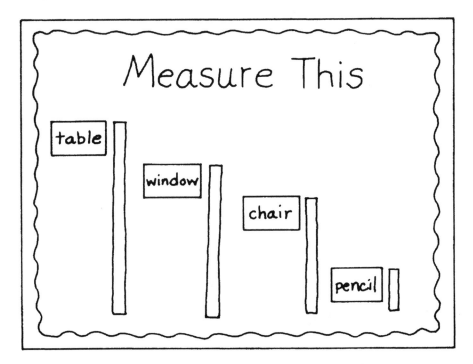

Extended Learning
Use 1" graph paper as a background for the bulletin board, and have students count and color the squares.

100 Days Hooray! Tally Chart

Materials

paper shapes

tagboard

black, red, and green pens

Skills Objective

Count to 100.

A **Tally Chart** allows students to keep track of data easily. Counting the days of school is a tradition in many kindergarten classrooms. A tally of days provides students with a visual guide of how our number system works.

1. On the first day of school, introduce the Count-Up Calendar. Print the numeral *1* on a paper shape. Attach the paper shape to a strip of tagboard, and place it on the wall of your classroom. The next school day, add a paper shape with the numeral *2* printed on it. Continue adding a shape for each school day.

2. Once five days have passed, begin with a new strip of tagboard. Use black ink for numbers *1–4*, red ink for each multiple of 5, and green ink for each multiple of 10 to reinforce number concepts.

3. Continue counting each school day up to 100. Use the Count-Up Calendar for counting activities throughout the year.

4. Hold a classroom celebration on the 100th day of school. Students might choose to make collages with 100 items, take a walk of 100 steps, or collect 100 cans of food for a food drive.

Extended Learning

Purchase a 100-piece jigsaw puzzle. Solve the puzzle beforehand. Number the pieces from 1 to 100 beginning with the corner and outside edge pieces, and moving inward. Reassemble the puzzle with your students by adding one numbered piece to the puzzle each day.

CHAPTER 2

Science

Sink or Float? Sectioned Chart

Skills Objective

Compare and contrast the properties of objects.

Students can use a **Sectioned Chart** to record data from experiments. In this activity, students discover the properties of materials and use a sectioned chart to record the results.

1. Lead students in a discussion about objects that float in water. Brainstorm a list of items that float and items that sink. Record their ideas on chart paper. Encourage them to reflect on how they know this information.

2. Tell students that they will get an opportunity to test their ideas. Show them a tub of water. Choose an object and think aloud as you hypothesize whether the item will sink or float: *I think this cotton ball will float because it is lightweight.* Drop the object into the water and observe it for a full minute. Demonstrate how to draw the item on the **Sink or Float? reproducible (page 30)**.

3. Organize students into partners. Give a tub of water, an assortment of objects to test, and two copies of the Sink or Float? reproducible to each pair. Have students take turns choosing an object and predicting whether it will sink or float. Invite them to draw or write their observations on the sectioned chart.

4. After students test all the items, discuss the results. Review the observations that students made before conducting their experiment, and talk about why items sink or float.

Extended Learning

Provide students with clay and aluminum foil. Instruct them to roll the items into a ball and see whether they float or sink. *(They sink.)* Then challenge them to find a way to make the items float. Discuss how shape affects buoyancy.

Materials

Sink or Float? reproducible

chart paper

tub of water

assorted objects for investigation (clay, aluminum foil, ice cube, crayon, sponge, cotton ball, cork, rock)

Sink or Float?

Directions: Choose an object and write its name. Place it in the water and watch. Does it sink or float? If it sinks, draw the object below the water line. If it floats, draw it above the water line. Do the same for three other objects.

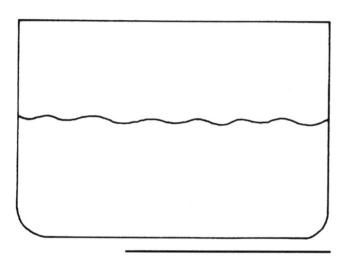

Object: _____

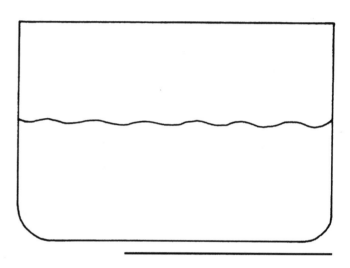

Object: _____

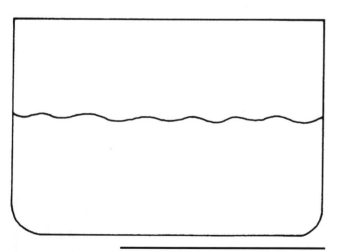

Object: _____

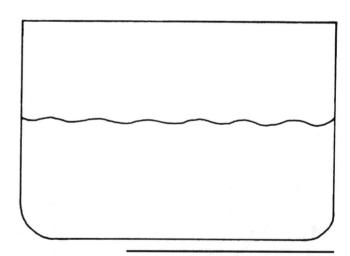

Object: _____

What's the Weather? Journal

Skills Objective
Observe and document daily weather changes.

Materials
What's the Weather? reproducible

A **Journal** provides students with the opportunity to record data over time. In this activity, students record their observations in a weather journal. As they monitor the weather, students use their senses to observe changes in the environment.

1. Lead students in a discussion about the day's weather. Ask them to tell how they know what the weather is like. Lead students to understand that they can use their five senses to learn about the weather. Review the five senses (sight, sound, touch, taste, smell) with students.

2. Brainstorm a list of words that describe the weather. List the ideas (*windy, cold, cloudy*) on the board. Make connections between these weather words and the five senses. With students' help, write symbols next to each word to indicate whether it is something that can be seen, touched, smelled, tasted, or heard.

3. Give students a copy of the **What's the Weather? reproducible (page 32)**. Explain that students will use their senses to observe the weather. (The sense of taste has been omitted from the reproducible.) Model how to use the journal page to record observations.

4. Have students record their observations on the reproducible for five days. At the end of the week, lead students in a discussion about their weather journals. Ask: *Why is it important to notice changes in the weather?*

Extended Learning
- Invite students to graph their weather data individually or as a class. Discuss which senses are most helpful in learning about the weather.

- Introduce the idea that scientists called *meteorologists* observe the weather and predict how it will change. Help students make sense of a television or newspaper weather report.

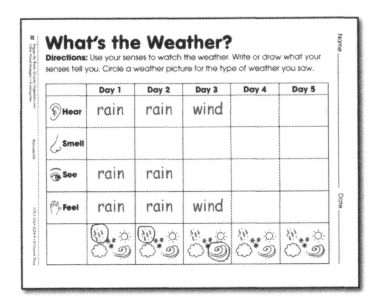

What's the Weather?
Directions: Use your senses to watch the weather. Write or draw what your senses tell you. Circle a weather picture for the type of weather you saw.

	Day 1	Day 2	Day 3	Day 4	Day 5
Hear	rain	rain	wind		
Smell					
See	rain	rain			
Feel	rain	rain	wind		

What's the Weather?

Directions: Use your senses to watch the weather. Write or draw what your senses tell you. Circle a weather picture for the type of weather you saw.

	Day 1	Day 2	Day 3	Day 4	Day 5
Hear					
Smell					
See					
Feel					

Reproducible

Colors in Nature: Sectioned Chart

Skills Objective

Collect and analyze natural specimens.

A **Sectioned Chart** helps organize information and images. In this activity, students use a sectioned chart to explore and note the attributes of natural items they collect on a nature walk.

1. Guide a class discussion about nature. Show them several objects, such as a penny, a leaf, a rock, and a spoon. Use plastic hoops or yarn circles to classify the items into two groups—objects from nature and objects not from nature.

2. Focus students' attention on the objects from nature. Identify the color of each object, and discuss the colors found most often in nature (e.g., *green, brown, red, orange, yellow*).

3. Invite students on a nature walk to collect small objects in a variety of colors. Before going on the walk, establish some guidelines. Remind students not to disturb living creatures. Ask them to make a circle with their thumb and forefinger and collect samples that are this size or smaller.

4. Give each student a plastic bag and instruct students to look for something green, something brown, and items of other colors. Have each student collect at least four samples.

5. Back in the classroom, give students a copy of the **Colors in Nature reproducible (page 34)**. Have them sort their samples according to color. Help students write the name and color of each sample and glue their items in place.

6. Display students' completed charts. Invite students to compare and contrast the objects and colors.

Extended Learning

- Make a list of the colors and items students found. Graph the items to see which color was found most often.

- Repeat this activity throughout the year to observe seasonal changes.

Materials

Colors in Nature reproducible

objects from nature (leaf, twig, rock)

objects not from nature (penny, pencil, spoon)

two plastic hoops

resealable plastic bags

glue

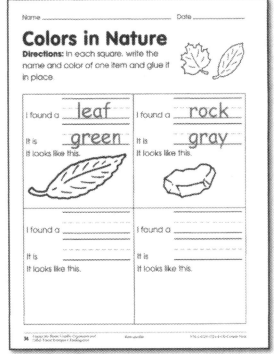

Colors in Nature

Directions: In each square, write the name and color of one item and glue it in place.

I found a _____
_ _ _ _ _ _ _ _ _ _ _ _ _ _ _ _
_____

It is _ _ _ _ _ _ _ _ _ _ _ _ _ _
_____

It looks like this.

I found a _____
_ _ _ _ _ _ _ _ _ _ _ _ _ _ _ _
_____

It is _ _ _ _ _ _ _ _ _ _ _ _ _ _
_____

It looks like this.

I found a _____
_ _ _ _ _ _ _ _ _ _ _ _ _ _ _ _
_____

It is _ _ _ _ _ _ _ _ _ _ _ _ _ _
_____

It looks like this.

I found a _____
_ _ _ _ _ _ _ _ _ _ _ _ _ _ _ _
_____

It is _ _ _ _ _ _ _ _ _ _ _ _ _ _
_____

It looks like this.

Be a Rock Star: Observation Form

Skills Objective
Analyze and compare rocks.

Materials
Be a Rock Star reproducible

rocks

magnifying glasses

plastic hoops or graphing mat

An **Observation Form** can help students gather and record consistent types of information about a variety of objects or specimens. The recorded data can then be compared and analyzed. In this investigation, students use a chart to analyze and describe rocks they find in their environment.

1. Explain to students that they will be learning about rocks. Their job is to find three or four rocks to study. If possible, lead students on a rock hunt around the school grounds. Or, have students collect rocks at home and bring them to school.

2. Once students have gathered an assortment of rocks, ask them to spread out the rocks on the floor and look at them. Encourage students to touch the rocks and notice their size, shape, and color. Give them magnifying glasses to examine the rocks.

3. Ask students to suggest categories for sorting the rocks. Using two plastic hoops or a graphing mat, sort the rocks according to size, shape, texture, color, or other attributes.

4. Have students each choose one rock to study, and give them a copy of the **Be a Rock Star reproducible (page 36)**. Explain that scientists write notes to record their observations. Model how to complete the reproducible using one of the rocks students brought to class.

5. Invite students to study the rock they selected and record notes on the reproducible. When they have finished sketching their rocks, have them exchange papers with a partner. Challenge students to find the rock that their partner described using information on the observation form.

6. Gather students for a discussion about the activity. Encourage them to tell what they learned about their rock and reflect on how taking notes helped them learn.

Extended Learning
Have partners use a balance scale to compare the weight of their rocks.

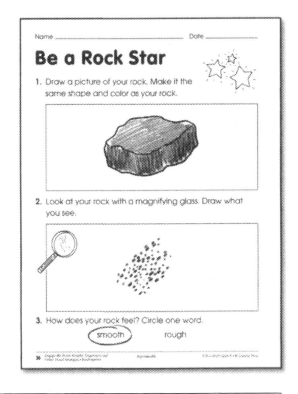

Be a Rock Star

1. Draw a picture of your rock. Make it the same shape and color as your rock.

2. Look at your rock with a magnifying glass. Draw what you see.

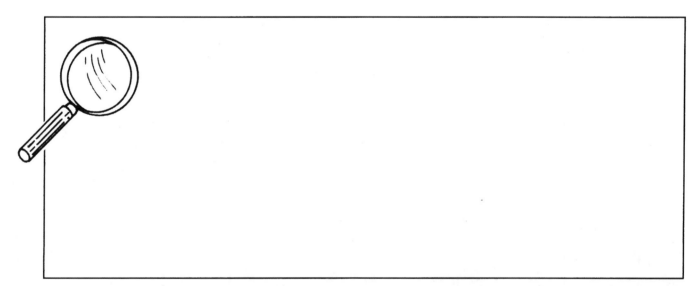

3. How does your rock feel? Circle one word.

smooth   rough

Living or Not Living? Two-Column Chart

Skills Objectives
Identify characteristics of living things.
Distinguish living things from nonliving things.

A **Two-Column Chart** displays items in an organized fashion and allows students to look for and compare information quickly and easily. In this activity, students use a two-column chart to better understand the distinction between living and nonliving things.

1. Show students a doll or action figure. Ask them to think about how the doll is like them and how it is different.

2. Draw a Venn diagram on the board. Label the first circle with the name of the doll. Label the other circle *Humans*, and label the intersecting section *Both*.

3. Ask students to think about characteristics of themselves and the doll. If a characteristic is unique to the doll, write it in the first circle. If the characteristic is unique to them, write it in the circle labeled *Humans*. If the characteristic is shared by both, write it in the intersecting section.

4. Ask students: *How can you tell when something is living? What do all living things need?* Lead them to understand that all living things need food, water, and air. Show students some picture cards, and ask them to classify the items as living or not living. Ask: *Does the item need food, water, and air?*

5. Divide the class into pairs, and give each pair a copy of the **Living or Not Living? reproducible (page 38)** and several magazines. Invite students to cut out pictures, sort them into the appropriate column on the page, and glue them in place.

6. Invite pairs to share their completed charts with the class. Encourage students to explain why they sorted the pictures into each category.

Extended Learning
Have pairs sort magazine pictures into categories of their own choosing. They might choose to sort pictures of animals by whether they have fur or don't have fur, or sort items by whether they can be found inside or outside. Encourage students to explain their choices.

Living or Not Living?

Directions: Which things are living? Which things are not living? Glue your pictures in the correct box.

 **Living**

 **Not Living**

Magnetic Attraction: Two-Column Chart

Skills Objective
Explore the properties of magnets.

A **Two-Column Chart** allows students to sort by two attributes. In this investigation, students will discover the properties of magnetic attraction and record their results in a two-column chart.

1. Show students a magnet. Ask them to explain what it is and how it is used. Write ideas on the board. Introduce the word *attract*. Invite students to predict which objects in the classroom will be attracted by the magnet. Test their predictions.

2. Tell students that they are going to discover what objects magnets pick up by conducting an experiment. Model how to test objects with the magnets, and write the results on the **Magnetic Attraction reproducible (page 40)**.

3. Divide students into pairs. Give each pair a magnet, a bag of items to test, and two copies of the Magnetic Attraction reproducible. Ask students to dump out the materials into a big pile and sort the objects into two piles using the magnet. Once students have sorted the materials, have them draw the results on the chart.

4. Gather students to discuss the results of their investigation. Have them look at the materials attracted to the magnet, and discuss what they have in common. *(They are metal.)* Point out that one part of the pencil is magnetic and another part is not. Discuss why the penny is not attracted to the magnet. *(Not all metals are attracted.)* Encourage students to share what they learned during the experiment.

Extended Learning
Have students work with more than one magnet at a time. Let them discover what happens when they put two magnets together.

Safety Note: Explain to students that they must never use a magnet near a computer. Supervise students' use of magnets to prevent damage to classroom computer equipment.

Materials
Magnetic Attraction reproducible

magnets

magnetic and nonmagnetic objects (paper clips, nails, aluminum foil, pennies, pencils, rubber bands)

resealable plastic bags

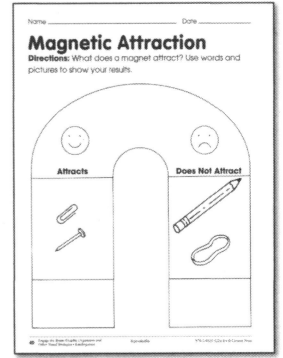

Magnetic Attraction

Directions: What does a magnet attract? Use words and pictures to show your results.

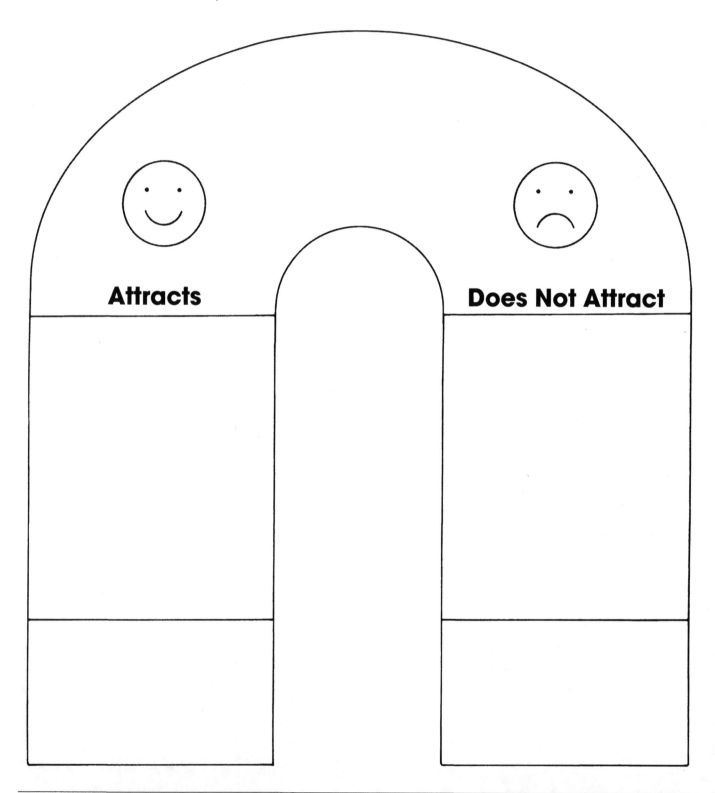

Attracts

Does Not Attract

Sky Watchers: Picture Chart

Skills Objective

Observe and record changes in the day and night sky.

A **Picture Chart** is a simple way for young students to record scientific discoveries. In this activity, students watch the sky and use a chart to record their observations.

A **Picture Chart** is a simple way for young students to record scientific discoveries. In this activity, students watch the sky and use a chart to record their observations.

Materials

Sky Watchers reproducible

chart paper

1. Lead students in a discussion about the sky. Ask them to brainstorm a list of things they can see in the sky and words that describe the sky. Use words and sketches to record their ideas on chart paper.

2. Explain that students can use their eyes to learn more about the sky. Take students outdoors to look at the daytime sky. (Caution them not to look directly at the sun.) Discuss how scientists make observations. Ask: *What objects did you see? Were they moving or standing still? Which objects were living? Which were machines? Which of these objects would you be able to see at night?*

3. Give students a copy of the **Sky Watchers reproducible (page 42)**. Have them use words and pictures to record in the big sun what they see in the daytime sky.

4. Invite students to take home their Sky Watchers reproducible to record in the big moon what they see in the nighttime sky. Send a letter home to parents and caregivers telling them how to assist their child in observing the nighttime sky.

5. Provide time for students to share and discuss their sky observations with the class. Bind the pages into a class book to add it to the classroom library for all to enjoy!

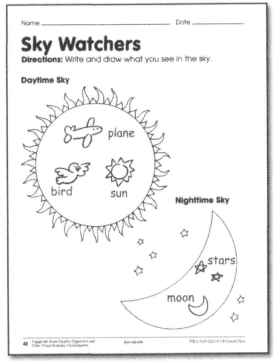

Sky Watchers

Directions: Write and draw what you see in the sky.

Daytime Sky

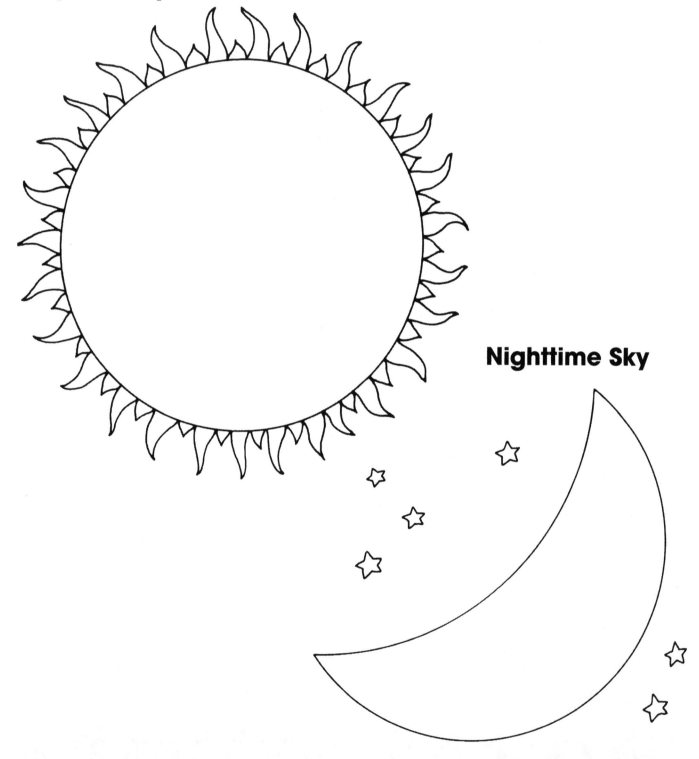

Nighttime Sky

Weather Wheel

Skills Objective
Observe and record weather conditions.

A **Wheel** displays facts or attributes associated with a single topic or concept. In this activity, a weather wheel provides students with a visual reminder of the day's weather. Each day, ask a volunteer to point the arrow to the day's weather.

1. Make a copy of the **Weather Wheel reproducible (below)**. Cut out the circle and glue it to a heavy piece of cardboard for added durability.

2. Glue the arrow to a heavy piece of cardboard and cut it out. Attach the arrow to the wheel by pushing a brad fastener through the center of the wheel.

Materials

Weather Wheel reproducible

glue

cardboard

brad fastener

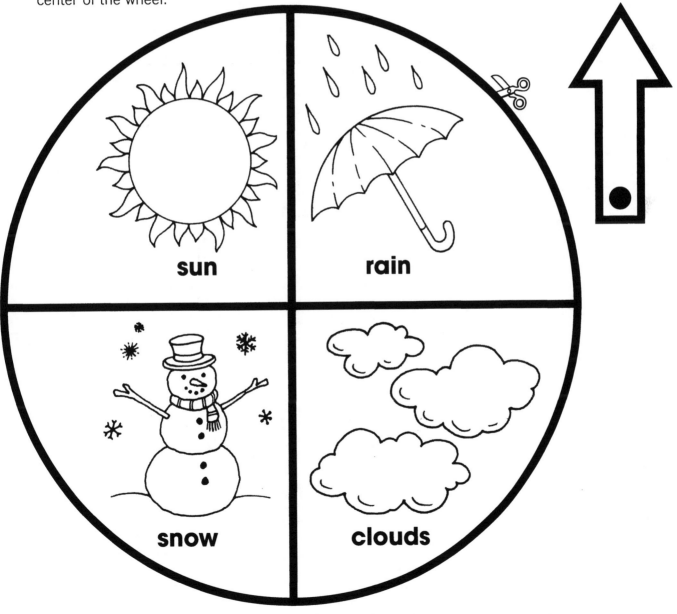

sun   rain

snow   clouds

CHAPTER 3

Social Studies

Then and Now: Timeline

Materials

Then and
Now Timeline
reproducible

baby doll

Skills Objective

Identify the past, present, and future.

A **Timeline** presents events in chronological order using a linear model. In this activity, students use a timeline as a visual tool to illustrate their understanding of past, present, and future.

1. Show students a baby doll. Discuss how a baby behaves and what it needs. Remind students that they were once babies.

2. Draw a horizontal line on the board. Explain that this is a timeline that shows how things change over time. Mark a point on the far left side and label it with the word *Baby*. Ask students to name things that they did when they were babies. List these ideas at the beginning of the timeline.

3. Remind students that they are no longer babies. Mark a point in the middle of the timeline and label it with the word *Now*. Encourage students to brainstorm things that they can do now that they did not do when they were babies. Add these ideas to the timeline.

4. Ask students what they would like to learn to do in the future. Mark another point on the far right side of the timeline and label it with the word *Future*. Discuss some of the things students might do when they grow up. Add these ideas to the timeline.

5. Invite students to complete the **Then and Now Timeline reproducible (page 45)** about their own past, present, and future. Encourage students to use words and pictures.

6. Have students meet in small groups to discuss their timelines. Compile the timelines into a group book, and invite students to reread the book at the end of the school year.

Then and Now Timeline

Directions: Use words and pictures to show what you did when you were a baby, what you can do now, and what you will do when you grow up.

Baby

Now

When I Grow Up

Class Address Book: Form

Materials

Address Book Form reproducible

telephone directory

overhead projector or chart paper

index cards

three-ring binder

Skills Objectives

Compile an address book.
Use a graphic organizer to represent data.

A **Form** provides a structure for recording information consistently from student to student, making the data easy to locate and read. In this activity, students record their address and phone number on a form to create a class address book. (Before starting this activity, be sure to obtain permission from parents for sharing personal information.)

1. Show students a telephone directory. Ask: *What is this book? What is it used for?* Read a few entries with students. Point out that the entries are alphabetized according to last name. Suggest that students make their own class directory.

2. Make a transparency of the **Address Book Form reproducible (page 47),** or copy it on chart paper. Demonstrate how to fill in the name, address, and phone number.

3. Prepare an index card with each student's name, address, and phone number. Place the index cards and multiple copies of the Address Book reproducible in the classroom writing center. Have students copy their name, address, and phone number on the reproducible and draw a picture of their face in the box beside their name.

4. Compile the pages and bind them in a three-ring binder. Place the binder in the dramatic play area, and invite students to incorporate it into their dramatic play.

Extended Learning

Discuss the 911 emergency number and the situations in which it is used.

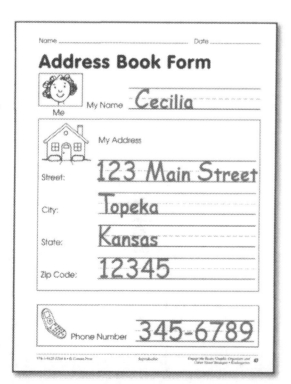

Name _____ Date _____

Address Book Form

Me

My Name _____
_ _ _ _ _ _ _ _ _ _ _ _ _ _ _ _ _ _
_____

My Address

Street: _____
_ _ _ _ _ _ _ _ _ _ _ _ _ _ _ _ _ _

City: _____
_ _ _ _ _ _ _ _ _ _ _ _ _ _ _ _ _ _

State: _____
_ _ _ _ _ _ _ _ _ _ _ _ _ _ _ _ _ _

Zip Code: _____

Phone Number _____
_ _ _ _ _ _ _ _ _ _ _ _ _ _ _ _ _ _

My Community: Concept Map

Materials

My Community reproducible

chart paper

Skills Objective

Identify aspects of a community.

A **Concept Map** is a useful tool for helping students gather, connect, and see how facts are related. In kindergarten, students develop and refine their understanding of community by investigating the ways in which people live together and help each other.

1. To begin your unit of study, write the word *community* on chart paper and ask students to define it. Guide students to understand that a community is a group of people who work together. Generate a list of communities to which students belong. These might include family, school, neighborhood, team, town, state, and church.

2. Give students a copy of the **My Community reproducible (page 49)**. Have students use words and pictures to describe their family, school, neighborhood, and town. Remind students that they can use the words and ideas on the class list to help them complete their concept maps.

3. After students have shared their community concept maps in small groups, save them in students' portfolios. Repeat this activity at the end of your community unit. Invite students to compare the two concept maps and think about what they have learned.

Extended Learning

Suggest that students work in small groups to build a community model using blocks.

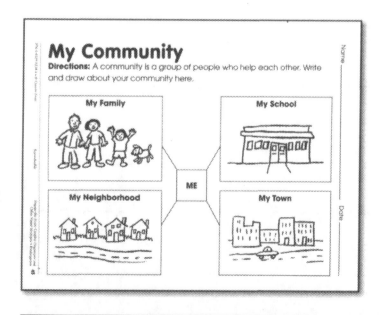

Name _____ Date _____

My Community

Directions: A community is a group of people who help each other. Write and draw about your community here.

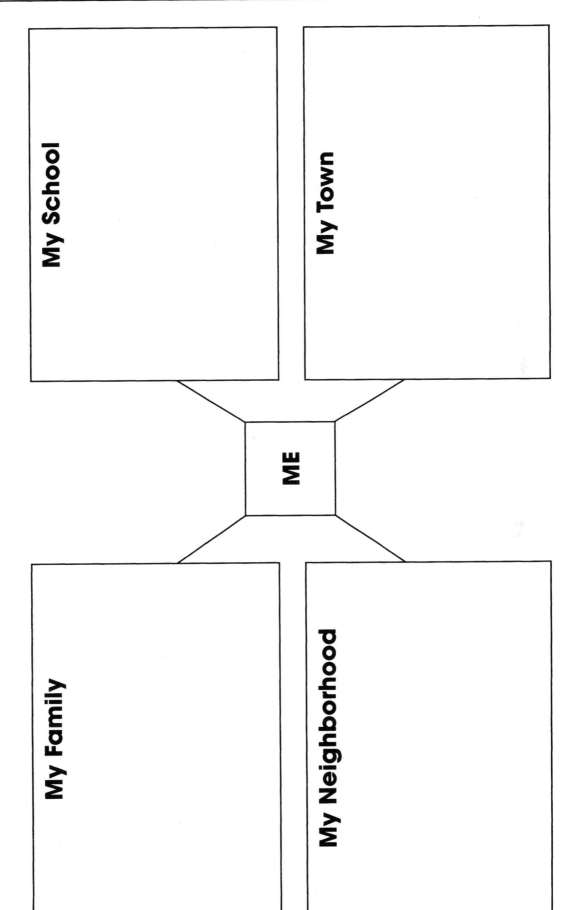

My School

My Town

ME

My Family

My Neighborhood

In the Neighborhood: K-N-L Chart

Materials

K-N-L Chart
reproducible

overhead projector
or chart paper

Skills Objective

Investigate neighborhood and community.

The **K-N-L Chart** is useful for helping students access prior knowledge, set a purpose for learning, and summarize what they have learned. In this activity, students use this strategy to launch an investigation of their neighborhood.

1. Make a transparency of the **K-N-L Chart reproducible (page 51)** or copy it onto chart paper. Review with students the communities to which they belong, including a neighborhood. Ask them to brainstorm what they know about their neighborhood. List their ideas in the "What I **K**now" column of the chart.

2. Then ask: *What do we need to know about our neighborhood?* Add these suggestions to the "What I **N**eed to Know" column of the chart. Together, brainstorm methods of gathering the needed information.

3. Give students a copy of the K-N-L Chart reproducible. Have them work in small groups to write or draw one thing they know about their neighborhood and one thing they need to know. Circulate among groups and assist students in writing as necessary.

4. At the conclusion of students' investigation, have them fill in the "What I **L**earned" column. Ask students: *Did you learn everything you need to know about the topic? Did your ideas change?* Invite students to share the information they learned and see if they can help each other with any unanswered questions.

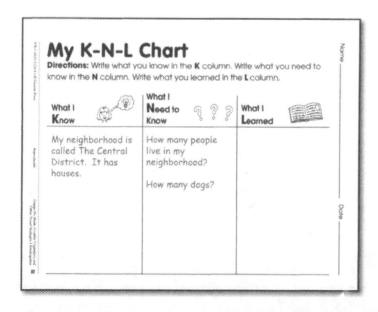

Name _____ Date _____

My K–N–L Chart

Directions: Write what you know in the **K** column. Write what you need to know in the **N** column. Write what you learned in the **L** column.

What I **K**now	What I **N**eed to Know	What I **L**earned

Getting There: Mind Map

Materials

Mind Map reproducible

construction paper

butcher paper

crayons or markers

scissors

yarn

Skills Objective

Create a collaborative mind map about transportation.

A **Mind Map** is a simple yet effective technique in which students use words, symbols, and drawings to record and clarify their understanding of a topic. In this activity, students create a collaborative mind map about transportation.

1. Ask students: *What is transportation?* Establish that transportation is a way of going from one place to another. Print the word *transportation* on a sheet of construction paper and place it in the center of a bulletin board.

2. Guide a discussion about different types of transportation. Ask students to think of main ideas related to this topic and share their ideas with the class. List some of their words and ideas on the board.

3. Give students a copy of the **Mind Map reproducible (page 53)**. Model how to use the pieces to express a main idea about transportation. Students should write words related to their main idea in the squares and draw a picture that shows their main idea in the circle. Invite them to look at the board to find words.

4. As students complete their mind map, have them cut out the shapes and write their name on the back of each piece. Arrange the mind map pieces on a transportation-themed bulletin board using yarn to connect the ideas.

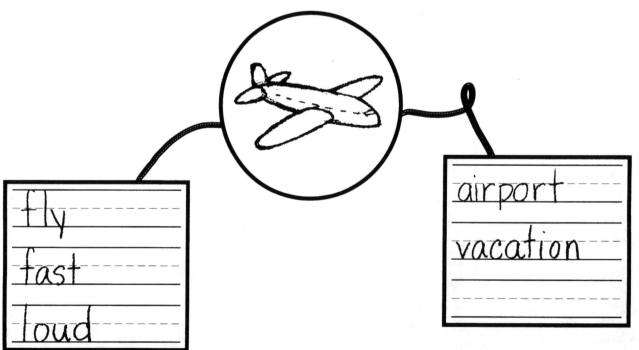

Mind Map

Directions: Draw a picture in the circle that shows your main idea. Write words that tell about your idea in the boxes.

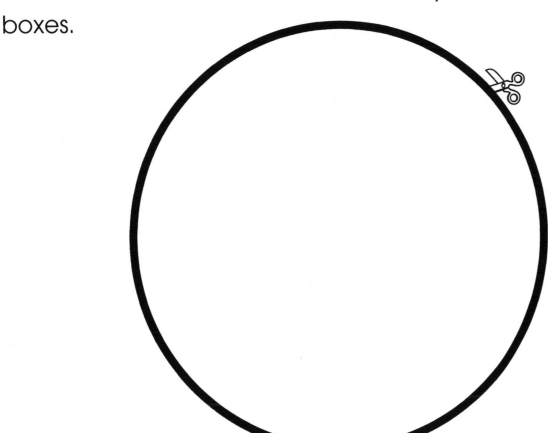

Cool Rules: Three-Column Chart

Materials

Rules Help Us reproducible

pictures of sports activities

chart paper

Skills Objectives

Understand the purpose of rules.

Define rules.

In this activity, a **Three-Column Chart** helps students generate and classify classroom rules. Classroom rules are more meaningful when students set the guidelines themselves.

1. Ask students: *What is a rule?* Discuss what it means to have rules and why rules are important.

2. Invite students to name some of the rules they know. If students have difficulty thinking of examples, show pictures of activities such as bike riding, going to the beach, or playing sports. Talk about the rules people must follow in these circumstances.

3. Ask students: *Do you think we need rules in our classroom? Why or why not?* Establish that classroom rules help students learn, stay safe, and get along. Explain that students can work together to write rules that will help make the classroom a safe, enjoyable place for everyone.

4. Write *Rules Help Us Learn* on the board. Have students brainstorm rules that fit this category. Repeat this procedure for *Rules Help Us Stay Safe* and *Rules Help Us Get Along*.

5. Copy the rules onto chart paper and display them in the classroom.

6. Give students a copy of the **Rules Help Us reproducible (page 55)**. Invite them to show what they have learned about rules and share their charts with the class.

Rules Help Us

Directions: Use words and pictures to show what you know about class rules.

Get Along	Stay Safe	Learn

Bird's Eye View: Map

Materials

Here's My Map reproducible

Me on the Map by Joan Sweeney

assorted maps

chart paper

variety of objects (action figures, play food, school supplies)

plastic trays

digital camera

Skills Objectives

Make a map.
Read simple maps.

Making and reading a **Map** challenges students to extend their visual thinking and interpret abstract representations. In this activity, students investigate maps before creating their own.

1. Read aloud *Me on the Map* by Joan Sweeney or another informational book about maps. Discuss with students why maps are important.

2. Explore examples of different maps from the book. Help students locate themselves on a map of their town, their country, or a globe. Point out the key on each map.

3. Look again at the room map in the book. Explain that the map shows what the room would look like from overhead. With students' help, draw a map of your classroom on chart paper.

4. Check for understanding. Point to locations on the map and have students find the corresponding locations in the classroom. Then point to areas in the classroom and have students find them on the map.

5. Divide the class into pairs. Give each pair a copy of the **Here's My Map reproducible (page 57)** and a plastic tray with several items on it. Demonstrate how to use the reproducible to draw a map of the items on the tray. As you model the activity, use words such as *up, down, left,* and *right.* Point out the direction key that shows which way the tray is pointing.

6. As students are working, take a digital photo of each tray. When students have completed their maps, collect the maps and show students the photos. Ask students to match the photos to the maps.

Here's My Map
Directions: Look at the tray. Draw a map of what you see.

Name _____ Date _____

Here's My Map

Directions: Look at the tray. Draw a map of what you see.

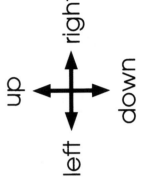

Places We Go: Map

Skills Objective

Make and use a map.

Making a **Map** requires that students understand how to view an area from an aerial perspective and organize what they see. In this activity, students work together to make and use a map of their school grounds.

1. Ask students to think back to their first day of school. Have them close their eyes as they recall how they found places, such as the lunchroom, the playground, and the bathroom.

2. Talk about how people find their way around unfamiliar places. Point out that maps help people find their way. Suggest that students make a map to help people find their way around the school.

3. Sketch an outline of the school building on chart paper. Remind students that a map shows what a place looks like from above. Ask them to imagine they are floating above the building and describe what they see below. Sketch these areas on the map. Have volunteers add details and label each area.

4. When the map is complete, mount it on posterboard and display it in the classroom. Each time the class returns from a trip outside, add a pushpin to the map to mark where students have been. At the end of the day, review students' movements by looking at the pushpins and recalling where the class went. Continue this activity for several days using different colored pushpins each day.

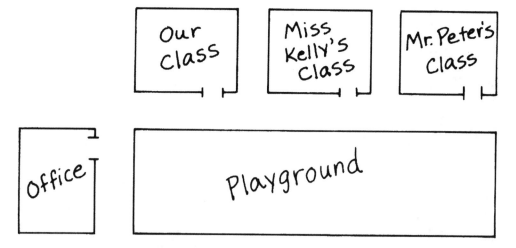

Extended Learning

Have students ask a parent or caregiver to help them make a map of their bedroom at home. Encourage them to label their maps and compare them in class.

I Need It! I Want It! Circle Chart

Skills Objective
Recognize and classify needs and wants.

A **Circle Chart** displays items in an organized fashion and allows students to compare information easily. In this activity, students use a circle chart to distinguish wants from needs.

1. Read aloud *Max's Dragon Shirt* by Rosemary Wells. Discuss the story and talk about what Max needed (*new pants*) and wanted (*a dragon shirt*). Ask students to explain the difference between wanting something and needing it.

2. Place two plastic hoops or yarn circles on the floor. Label one hoop *Wants* and the other hoop *Needs*. Give one magazine picture to each student.

3. Invite students to take turns showing their picture to the class and tell whether it is a want or a need. Then have them place their picture in the corresponding hoop.

4. Give students a copy of the **Wants and Needs reproducible (page 60)**. Have students use magazine pictures, drawings, and words to show things they need and things they want.

5. Invite students to share their work in small groups. Ask students to explain why they categorized the pictures as they did.

Extended Learning
Help students sort the pictures in each hoop into other categories, such as food, shelter, and clothing.

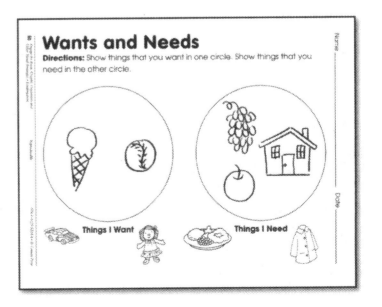

Wants and Needs

Directions: Show things that you want in one circle. Show things that you need in the other circle.

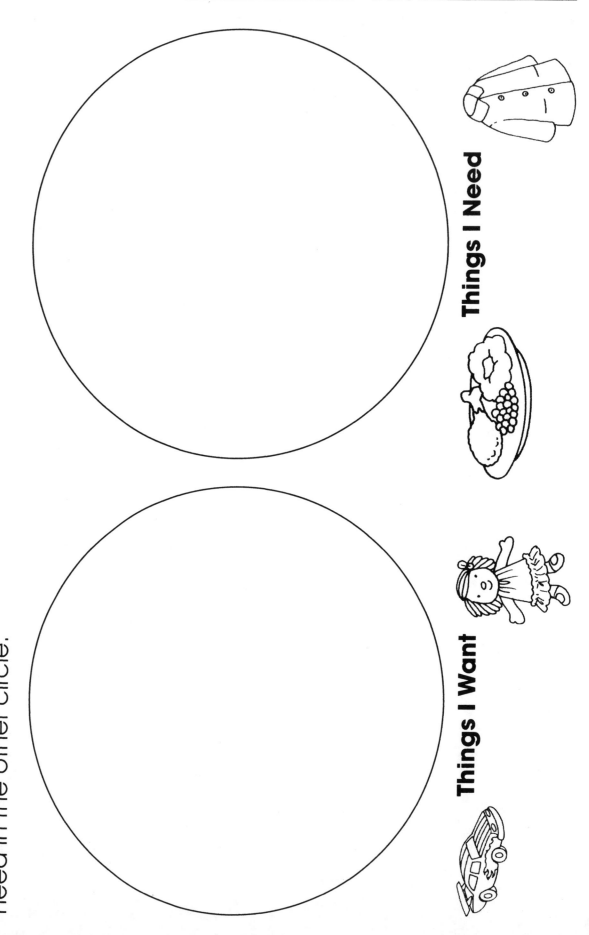

Things I Need

Things I Want

Transportation Museum: Three-Dimensional Display

Skills Objectives
Understand the purpose and characteristics of a museum.
Create a transportation display.

Materials
transportation-related items

masking tape

index cards

A **Three-Dimensional Display** includes a variety of objects that add interest and dimension to a presentation of ideas. In this activity, students create a transportation museum by selecting, arranging, and labeling artifacts in a display.

1. Ask students to share what they know about museums. If they have visited a museum, encourage them to recall what they saw and did during their visit. If not, explain to students that a museum is a place where people can go to look at and learn about things from history and around the world. Point out that there are many different kinds of museums, such as art museums, science museums, history museums, and transportation museums.

2. Tell students that they will create their own transportation museum in the classroom. Explain that in a museum, the things on display are called *artifacts*. The person who chooses the artifacts is called a *curator*. In your classroom transportation museum, all students will get a chance to be curators.

3. Discuss the artifacts students might include in their museum and brainstorm a list of ideas. Remind students that their museum might include toy vehicles, drawings, photographs, or stories about transportation.

4. Send home a note explaining the activity and asking each student to bring one or two items that could be displayed in the transportation museum. As students bring in artifacts, use masking tape to label each one.

5. Discuss different ways of organizing the collected transportation artifacts. When students have decided how to organize their museum collection, help them plan a display. Have students arrange the items on tables around the room. Provide index cards so students can label the artifacts with their name and the name of the item.

6. Hold a "grand opening" and invite guests from other classrooms to visit the museum. Encourage students to give guided tours of their museum and answer questions about the artifacts.

Extended Learning

- Have students verbally record descriptions of the items or transportation stories and experiences. Include these recordings in the display.

- Use a digital camera to photograph museum items. Download the photos and help students create a slideshow about transportation. Prompt students to write or dictate their reflections on learning into a journal.

CHAPTER 4

Language Arts

Picture Walk: Picture Chart

Skills Objectives

Make predictions about a book based on its illustrations.
Read to confirm predictions.

Materials

Picture Walk
reproducible

overhead projector

picture book

A **Picture Chart** organizes information in a visual way. In this activity, students take a "picture walk" as a pre-reading activity while recording their predictions, thoughts, and questions about a story.

1. Make a transparency of the **Picture Walk reproducible (page 64)**, and place it on the overhead.

2. Show students the front and back cover of a picture book. Read the title and the name of the author. Ask students: *What do you see on the cover?* List their ideas in the "What I See" path on the transparency.

3. Ask students: *What do you think the book might be about after looking at the title and illustration on the cover?* Record their ideas in the "What I Think" path on the transparency.

4. Ask students: *What do you wonder after looking at the cover?* Record questions in the "What I Wonder" path on the transparency.

5. Repeat this process with each picture spread in the book asking students all three questions and recording their ideas on the transparency.

6. After completing the picture walk for the entire book, read the entries on the chart with students. Then read the book. Look back at the chart so students can reflect on their predictions. Ask students what clues helped them make predictions and what parts of the book surprised them.

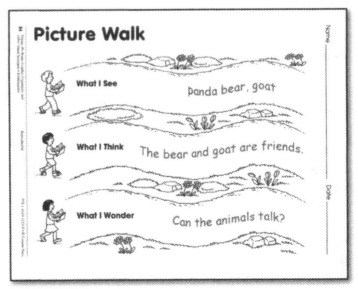

Name _____ Date _____

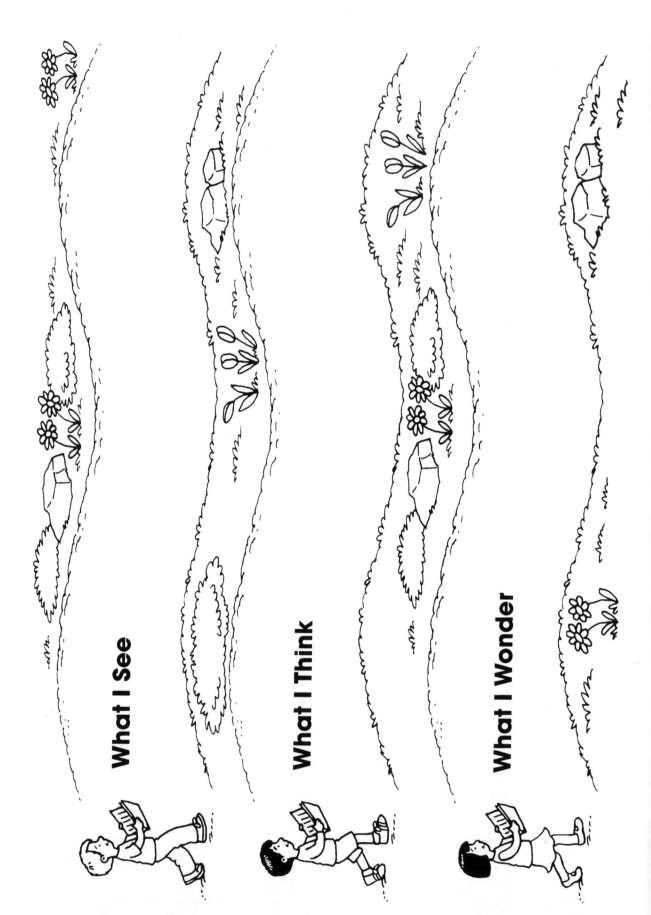

Picture Walk

What I See

What I Think

What I Wonder

 Engage the Brain: Graphic Organizers and Other Visual Strategies • Kindergarten   978-1-4129-5224-8 • © Corwin Press

Real or Make-Believe? T-Chart

Skills Objectives
Identify elements of fantasy.
Distinguish between real and make-believe.

Materials
Real or
Make-Believe?
reproducible

The Three Little Pigs
by Patricia Seibert

chart paper

A **T-Chart** helps students sort ideas into two categories. In this activity, students use a T-chart to distinguish between real and make-believe. As students discover different genres of literature, they begin to understand that certain stories could never really happen.

1. Read aloud a make-believe story, such as *The Three Little Pigs* by Patricia Seibert. Before reading, ask students to think about whether the story is real or make-believe. Encourage them to look and listen for events that could not happen in real life.

2. After reading the story, talk about the animals' actions in the story. Ask students: *Do you think this story could really happen, or do you think it is make-believe?* Encourage students to give reasons for their responses. Record their ideas on chart paper.

3. Give students a copy of the **Real or Make-Believe? reproducible (page 66)**. Ask them to describe the characters they are comparing, in this case, pigs. Instruct students to use words and pictures to express their understanding of real and make-believe.

4. Encourage students to think about why it is important to know the difference between things that are real and things that are not.

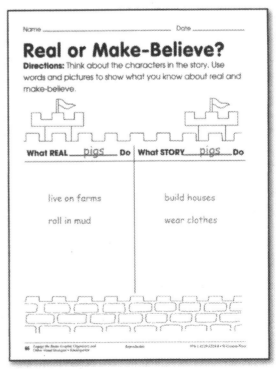

Real or Make-Believe?

Directions: Think about the characters in the story. Use words and pictures to show what you know about real and make-believe.

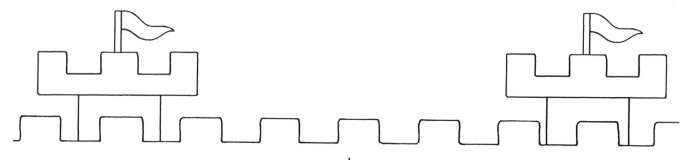

What REAL _____ Do | **What STORY _____ Do**

Story Steps: Sequence Chart

Skills Objective
Identify story sequence.

Identifying story sequence is one of the first steps in understanding story structure. A **Sequence Chart** helps students focus on the beginning, middle, and end of a story.

1. Explain to students that in a story, something happens first, something happens next, and something happens last. Ask them to listen as you read aloud *Lilly's Purple Plastic Purse* by Kevin Henkes.

2. Make a transparency of the **Story Steps reproducible (page 68)**. Model how to fill in the major story events. Think aloud, referring back to the book as needed to verify the steps in the story, for example: *I remember that at the beginning of the story, Lilly and her grandma bought a purple plastic purse. Does anyone remember what happened next?*

3. Give students a copy of the Story Steps reproducible. Have students draw pictures and write words to record what happened first, next, and last.

4. When students have completed their sequence charts, have them meet in small groups to discuss the story. Encourage them to refer to their drawings as they retell the beginning, middle, and end of the story.

Extended Learning
Have students form groups of three and take turns acting out the beginning, middle, and end of the story.

Materials
Story Steps reproducible

Lilly's Purple Plastic Purse by Kevin Henkes

overhead projector

Story Steps

Directions: Think about the steps in a story. Draw what happened in the beginning, middle, and end.

Story Title: _____

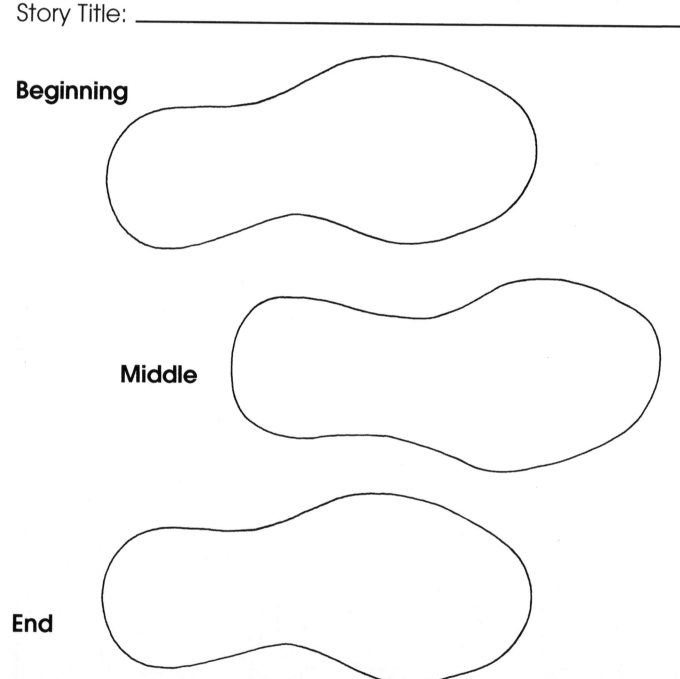

Beginning

Middle

End

What Happened and Why?
Cause-and-Effect Chart

Skills Objective
Identify cause and effect.

A **Cause-and-Effect Chart** helps students see the relationships among story events. Identifying cause and effect helps students better understand stories as well as topics in other subject areas, such as science, social studies, and math.

1. Inform students that when they read a story, it is important to think about not only *what* happens, but also *why* it happens.

2. Read aloud *If You Give a Mouse a Cookie* by Laura Joffe Numeroff or another book with clear cause-and-effect relationships. After reading, begin a discussion of the story by asking: *What happened first? What happened after the mouse got the cookie? Why did the mouse want some milk?* Establish that the mouse wanted milk because the cookie made him thirsty.

3. Draw two boxes on the board, with an arrow pointing from the first box to the second box. Label the first box *What Happened?* and the second box *Why?* Write the first event from the story and why it happened in the chart.

4. Continue asking volunteers to recall what happened in the story. Record their suggestions in new boxes. Point out how one event leads to another. Make sure students understand the concepts of *what happened* and *why*.

5. Give students a copy of the **What and Why? reproducible (page 70)**. Ask them to choose a favorite scene from the story and use the graphic organizer to draw an illustration explaining what happened and why. Encourage students to label their drawings. Remind them that they can use words and ideas from the class chart.

6. Have students refer to their cause-and-effect chart as they retell the story to a partner. Encourage them to use the word *because* in their retelling.

What and Why?

Directions: Draw pictures and write words to show what happened and why.

_____
- -

Story Title: _____

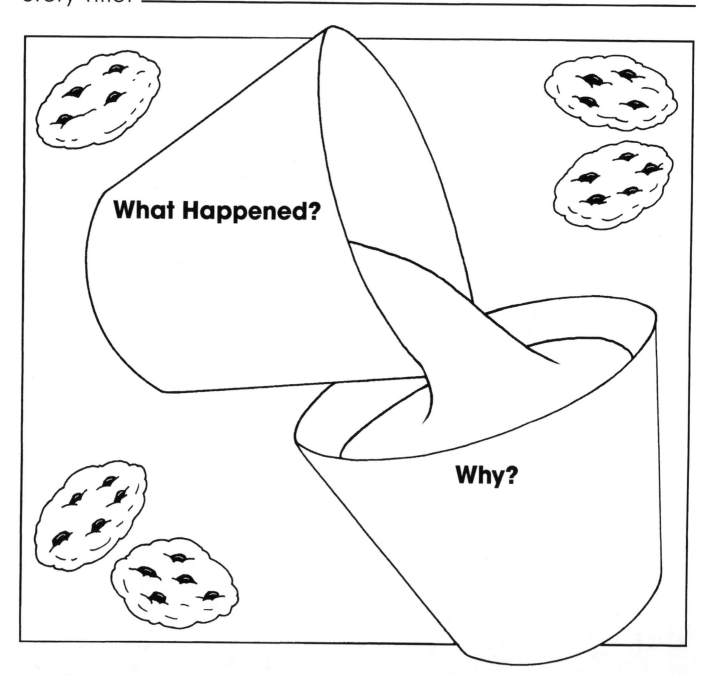

What Happened?

Why?

Count It Out: Segmenting Mat

Skills Objective
Identify and count the number of words in a sentence.

Materials
Count the Parts reproducible

counters (beans, pennies, paperclips)

A **Segmenting Mat** provides a workspace for students to count "parts." The parts may be syllables, sounds, or letters. In this activity, students focus on word awareness by counting the words in a sentence.

1. Draw four boxes on the board. Say a short sentence aloud, such as: *My dog can swim.* Draw an *X* in each box as you say each word. Repeat the activity, and invite student volunteers to draw the *X*s in the boxes.

2. Give each student a **Count the Parts reproducible (page 72)** and a set of counters.

3. Say another sentence aloud, such as: *How are you today?* Have students place one counter in a box for each word they hear. Remind students to work from left to right.

4. Once students have filled the boxes, have them repeat the sentence and point to the counters as they say the words.

5. Continue with new sentences. Once students are familiar with this activity, have them suggest sentences for their classmates to segment.

Name _____ Date _____

Count the Parts

Directions: Place one counter in each box for each word you hear.

Engage the Brain: Graphic Organizers and Other Visual Strategies • Kindergarten   Reproducible   978-1-4129-5224-8 • © Corwin Press

Word Wheel: Wheel

Skills Objectives
Increase vocabulary.
Connect words to concepts.

Materials
Word Wheel
reproducible

A **Wheel** displays facts or attributes associated with a single topic or concept. In this activity, students use a word wheel to improve vocabulary and their understanding of the concepts words represent.

1. Draw a word wheel on the chalkboard using the **Word Wheel reproducible (page 74)** as a guide. Explain to students that they can use the wheel to show their understanding of a word.

2. Write a topic, such as *Pets* in the center of the word wheel. Ask six volunteers to each name a type of pet. Write their responses in the sections of the word wheel. Add drawings or symbols to represent each type of pet.

3. Give students a copy of the Word Wheel reproducible. Have them make their own word wheels using a topic from a current unit of study or a topic of their choice.

4. Encourage students to use books and other sources to find examples of their topic. Point out that students can use words, pictures, or symbols to fill each section of the wheel.

5. Have students share their word wheels in small groups. Display their work at the classroom writing center.

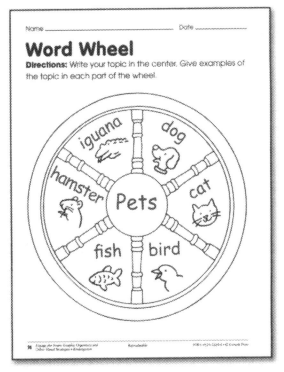

Word Wheel

Directions: Write your topic in the center. Give examples of the topic in each part of the wheel.

Print Walls: Word Wall

Skills Objectives
Categorize words by their initial letter.
Recognize rhyming words.
Connect initial consonant sounds with letters.

Materials
tagboard or colored
construction paper

The **Word Wall**, a class word bank, is a central feature in many elementary classrooms. To adapt this strategy for kindergarten, focus on words that are meaningful and useful for young learners. Try one or more of the following word wall variations.

Name Wall
Print students' names on strips of tagboard or colored construction paper. Categorize the names by first letter, number of letters, number of syllables, or other characteristics, and place them on the word wall.

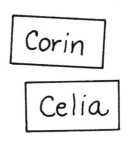

Print Wall
Ask students to bring in items with print from home. These might include food packages, magazine covers, or other examples of text. Ask students to read the text and place it on the wall according to its initial letter.

Alphabet Word Wall

Use the letters of the alphabet as labels for this word wall. Each week, read a different poem or song. Select a few vocabulary words from the poem, print them on tagboard or construction paper, and add them to the wall under the appropriate letter. For example, select the words *cow, moon,* and *spoon* from the nursery rhyme "Hey, Diddle, Diddle." Use the Alphabet Wall as a resource for a variety of phonics activities. For example:

- Read the words on the word wall chorally, emphasizing the initial letter and sound.

- Read three words from the word wall aloud, and ask students to identify the two that begin with the same letter.

- Reread the rhyme, pausing to allow students to find the word on the word wall.

- Play a guessing game. Give clues such as: *I'm thinking of a word that starts with the sound /m/. It's something you can see at night.* (moon)

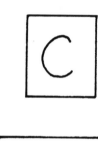

Story Retelling: Visual Props

Skills Objective
Retell stories using props.

Visual Props support young storytellers by providing a concrete framework for organizing information. In these activities, students build comprehension by retelling stories using drawings, puppets, and fingerplays.

Five-Finger Retelling
After reading aloud a story to students, model how to retell the story in your own words. Remind students that a story retelling should answer five questions:

Who was the story about?
Where did the story happen?
What happened at the beginning of the story?
What happened in the middle?
What happened at the end?

Invite students to retell the story to an adult partner. Suggest that they count on five fingers to remember the five important questions.

Puppet Play

Simple props, such as stick puppets, make it easy for students to demonstrate the actions of story characters. To make stick puppets, create illustrations on heavy paper and glue them to craft sticks. Or, attach a piece of Velcro to the back of each figure to make flannel board characters.

1. Read a book aloud to students.

2. Retell the story using the puppets. Pause to ask: *What happened next? Then what happened?*

3. Invite pairs of students to retell the story using the puppets. Suggest that students each choose a certain character to play. Remind them to include the important parts of the story.

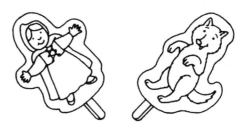

Chalk Talk

A Chalk Talk is a retelling strategy in which students draw pictures to represent a story while they talk about it. Chalk Talks are ideal for building students' oral language skills and sense of story elements. When students work with chalk, they can easily add to and revise their stories.

1. Model for students how to retell a story with which they are familiar. As you tell the story, quickly sketch the characters and key events on the board.

2. Invite students to work in small groups to retell and draw stories at the chalkboard. As students tell the stories, circulate, ask questions, and make comments.

3. Invite students to conduct Chalk Talks with their families. Send home a note suggesting that students tell stories to their families while drawing pictures with paper and pencil.

Color-Coded Words: Word Cards

Skills Objective
Isolate and identify vowel sounds.

Word Cards allow students to move and rearrange words, which turns a word study task into an engaging hands-on activity. In this activity, students use color-coded words to isolate and identify vowel sounds.

1. Make a set of color-coded word cards for each vowel sound students are studying. Print each word on an index card in black marker. Use a contrasting color, such as red, to print the vowels.

2. Begin by using cards with only one vowel sound. Display one word card (*hen*), and have students respond by saying the vowel sound (*/e/*). Repeat with the other cards in the set.

3. Continue displaying cards until students can confidently identify the vowel sound.

4. Display the cards again. This time, have students identify the sound and then read the word (*/e/*, *pen*).

5. Place the cards in the classroom literacy center for independent practice.

Puzzle Words: Word Cards

Materials

index cards

scissors

envelopes

crayons or markers

Skills Objectives

Construct words using letters.

Match text with pictures to create word meaning.

In this activity, students create word card puzzles to help them see how words are constructed. These **Word Cards** allow students to move and rearrange letters to explore parts of words.

1. Print a word on an index card, leaving space between the letters. Ask students to read the word. Cut apart the letters into interlocking pieces.

2. Give each puzzle piece to a different student. Have students work together to rebuild the word. Ask them to read the word and blend the sounds together.

3. Give each student an index card with a word written on it and an envelope. Instruct students to read the word on their card and draw a related picture on the envelope. Have them cut between the letters on the card pattern to make puzzle pieces, and then store the pieces in the envelope.

4. Have students form small groups, trade envelopes, and solve each other's puzzles. Keep the puzzle envelopes in the classroom reading center for students to work with during free time.

CHAPTER 5

Physical Education, Art, and Music

Watch Me Jump! Bar Graph

Skills Objectives
Create various ways of jumping.
Measure distance using nonstandard units of measure.

A **Bar Graph** can help young students measure accomplishments. Graphs are especially helpful for primary students because of their concrete nature. In this activity, kindergarteners can take pride in what their growing bodies can do.

1. Ask students to demonstrate various ways they can jump or hop, such as with two feet, on one foot, backwards, sideways, and twisting. As students demonstrate, list their ideas on the board.

2. Discuss the various things and ways we measure. Suggest that students measure how far they can jump.

3. Make a starting line on the floor with tape. Place several identical wooden blocks end-to-end to create a measuring line. Draw the same amount of blocks on the board.

4. Have a volunteer jump forward from the tape starting line. As a class, count the blocks to determine how far the student jumped. Record the results by coloring in the matching number of blocks on the board.

5. Give students a copy of the **Watch Me Jump! reproducible (page 82)**. Then have students work in small groups to jump in four different ways and record their results.

6. Discuss the results as a class. Ask students: *Which style of jumping resulted in the longest jumps? Which style of jumping is the most fun? How does a graph help us understand how we jump?*

Materials
Watch Me Jump! reproducible
tape
blocks

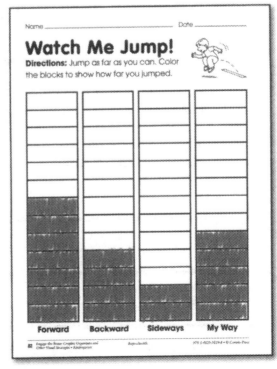

Name _____ Date _____

Watch Me Jump!

Directions: Jump as far as you can. Color the blocks to show how far you jumped.

| **Forward** | **Backward** | **Sideways** | **My Way** |

 Engage the Brain: Graphic Organizers and Other Visual Strategies • *Kindergarten*   Reproducible   978-1-4129-5224-8 • © Corwin Press

Step in Shape: Movement

Skills Objectives
Review shape and color concepts.
Follow directions.
Use a variety of locomotor skills.

Materials
colored tape

plastic cones

Movement provides extrasensory input to the brain and enhances memory for learning. In this activity, students follow pathways on the floor as they develop locomotor skills and review shape and color concepts.

1. Use colored tape and plastic cones to make eight to ten shape or line patterns on the floor. The shapes and patterns must be large enough for students to follow with their footsteps. Shape and line patterns may include:

square	straight line
circle	zigzag line
triangle	dotted line
rectangle	double line
oval	diamond

2. Give each shape or line pattern a name, and designate each as a station. Walk students from station to station as you introduce each one.

3. Assign each pair of students to begin at a different station. Call out locomotor directions, such as: *tiptoe, walk slowly, skip forward, skip backward,* or *hop.*

4. After each movement, invite pairs to rotate to another movement station. Provide another set of locomotor directions for students to follow.

5. Once students are familiar with this activity, add more complex directions, such as: *Jump if your path has three sides. Skip if your path is round.*

Extended Learning
- Encourage volunteers to give movement directions for the class to follow.

- Instead of naming actions, ask students to imitate animals by moving like a monkey, a puppy, a kangaroo, or a duck.

Healthy Hands: Sequence Chart

Materials

Healthy Hands reproducible

hand-washing supplies (sink, soap, towel)

Skills Objective

Learn how to wash hands properly to reduce the spread of germs.

A **Sequence Chart** displays information in a sequential order so students can recall a process. This sequence chart includes pictures to help young students comprehend text. It also works as a visual reminder for students learning how to wash properly.

1. Lead students in a discussion about germs. Explain that germs can cause people to get sick. Tell students: *Germs are very tiny and too small for us to see. When we touch things, we can get germs on our hands.* Inform them that the best way to get rid of germs is to wash our hands with soap and water.

2. Ask students: *How long should we wash our hands?* Explain that we need to wash our hands for at least 30 seconds. Have students watch the second hand of a clock while singing a song that lasts approximately 30 seconds, such as "The Alphabet Song" or "Happy Birthday." Remind them to sing one of these songs as they wash their hands to be sure they are washing for the right amount of time.

3. Show students a copy of the **Wash Your Hands reproducible (page 85)**. Read the steps with students, and demonstrate how to follow the directions as you wash your own hands. Have students sing "The Alphabet Song" or "Happy Birthday" to remind you how long to wash.

4. Check for understanding and confirm that students can identify the steps on the sequence chart.

5. Post the reproducible over the classroom sink, and invite students to follow the steps on the chart as they wash their hands throughout the day.

Extended Learning

- Allow students to take home their charts to post over the bathroom sink.

- Photocopy the pictures from the sign, cut them out, and have students sequence the steps.

Wash Your Hands

1. Turn on warm water.

2. Soap.

3. Scrub and sing.

4. Rinse.

5. Turn off water.

6. Dry.

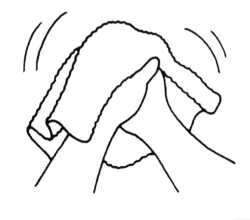

My Body Moves: Labeled Diagram

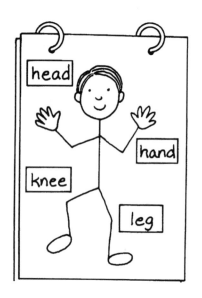

Materials

chart paper

index cards

Skills Objectives

Identify body parts.

Recognize body part functions.

A **Labeled Diagram** includes an illustration with labels to identify its parts. In this activity, a labeled diagram makes learning the names and functions of body parts more concrete and engaging.

1. Share the following action chant with students. Encourage them to join in and demonstrate how to move each body part.
   Teacher: *Let me see you move your head.*
   Student: *This is how I move my head.* (Moves head.)
   Teacher: *Let me see you move your nose.*
   Student: *This is how I move my nose.* (Scrunches up nose.)

2. Add verses for other body parts, such as ears, eyes, mouth, shoulders, elbows, chest, hands, fingers, knees, legs, feet, and toes, using the same format.

3. Draw a large stick figure on chart paper. Ask students to name the body parts they see on the stick figure. Print each word on a separate index card.

4. Distribute the word cards to students. Challenge students to read their word card with help from their classmates. Tape the card to the corresponding location on the body diagram. Ask students to read the word and point to the corresponding part of their own body.

5. Repeat this activity over a period of time so each student has an opportunity to label the body parts.

Extended Learning

- Play a guessing game about body parts. Ask students: *What part of the body do you use to eat an apple?* Have students point to an appropriate body part on the chart. Challenge students to name more than one body part for each action.

- Once students have mastered these "outside" body parts, make word cards for "inside" parts, such as heart, stomach, and lungs. Include a drawing on each card.

Collage Recipe: Rebus Chart

Skills Objectives
Follow directions independently.
Create a collage using specified materials.

Rebus Charts offer students a visual display of information without a lot of text to read. Rebus charts provide students with a visual reminder of a project's directions to promote independent work habits. Both open-ended and step-by-step projects are adaptable to this format.

1. Select materials that students will use to create a collage. Glue these materials to chart paper to make a rebus "recipe chart."

2. Ask students: *What is a collage?* If students are unfamiliar with this term, explain that a collage is a picture made by gluing different items together.

3. Show the chart to students. Explain that this is a list of materials for a collage similar to a list of ingredients in a recipe. Point out that the chart doesn't show how to make the collage. Each artist will figure out his or her own way of combining the materials to make a picture.

4. Check for understanding. Make sure students know what a collage is and understand the assignment.

5. Display the chart in the art center, and invite students to follow the rebus instructions to choose the selected collage materials. Provide time for students to arrange the collage materials in different ways before they glue them to their paper.

6. Encourage students to compare their collages in small groups. Discuss how each person used the same materials to make an original piece of art.

Materials
chart paper

collage materials (paper shapes in assorted colors and sizes, pipe cleaners, cotton balls)

construction paper

glue

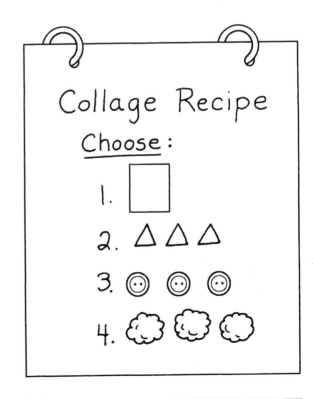

Our Quilt: Bulletin Board Display

Materials

The Keeping Quilt by Patricia Polacco

drawing paper

art supplies

wrapping paper or wallpaper cut into 2" strips

Skills Objectives

Understand how quilts are made.
Participate in a collaborative art project.

A **Bulletin Board Display** is an ideal way to highlight student artwork and integrate it into classroom instruction. Student-art displays inspire and reward young artists!

1. Read aloud a book about quilts, such as *The Keeping Quilt* by Patricia Polacco. Talk with students about the qualities of quilts. Explain that quilts are made from individual pieces stitched together make one beautiful piece of art.

2. Give each student a piece of drawing paper and some art supplies. Invite students to draw a picture that shows them doing something they enjoy with their family. Then have them write or dictate a description to match the illustration. It can be a label, a phrase, or a sentence.

3. When students have finished their pictures, invite them to frame their art with strips of wallpaper or wrapping paper.

4. Display student drawings in a quilt-like fashion on a bulletin board.

Art in Motion: Drawing

Skills Objectives
Learn about the art style of Keith Haring.
Experiment with music and movement.
Draw action figures.

Movement offers students the opportunity to act out a concept. In this activity, some students move to music and act as models, while other students use Keith Haring's art style to draw them. Haring uses bold lines and action figures to portray messages of energy and unity. Students will mimic Haring's style while **Drawing** their visual representations.

Materials
print reproductions of Keith Haring's work

lively music

CD or cassette player

drawing paper

art supplies

1. Show students examples of Haring's work. Ask: *What are these characters doing? How do we know they are moving?* Focus students' attention on the movement lines Haring uses for his dancing figures.

2. Divide the class into two groups. Have one group dance to lively music while the other group draws the dancers. As students draw, encourage them to think about how the dancers are moving and how they can show that in their drawings.

3. Invite groups to trade roles. When students have completed their drawings, display their work around the classroom.

4. As students encounter other artwork and picture book illustrations, encourage them to notice whether the characters appear to be moving or standing still.

Still Life: Concrete Model

Materials

paint reproductions of still life paintings

still life props

painting supplies

Skills Objectives

Understand the attributes of still life paintings.
Create a still life painting.

A **Concrete Model** can help students make connections between real life and representations of real life, such as a piece of artwork. A still life, a picture of inanimate objects, leads students to consider form and composition. In this activity, students observe and create still life paintings.

1. Ask students what the word *still* means. Explain that one meaning for the word *still* is *motionless*. Have students demonstrate this meaning. Ask: *Can you show me how to sit still?*

2. Introduce the term *still life*, and show students several examples of still life paintings. Explain that a still life shows things that people like to look at or use. Compare and contrast the shapes, colors, and subjects of the paintings.

3. Propose recreating a still life composition by arranging props on a table. Think aloud as you group the props in a similar arrangement to one of the paintings. Use words such as *next to, above, below, beside, close,* and *far.*

4. Place the still life prints and props in the art center for students to investigate.

5. Provide painting materials and props at the art center. Encourage students to paint their own still life painting using the props of their choice. Have them name their paintings before displaying them in a classroom gallery.

Farm Fun: Hand Signals

Skills Objective
Incorporate sign language into a familiar song.

Hand Signals are a visual strategy to engage students' brains. In this activity, students use sign language with verses of a familiar song.

1. Sing a familiar song such as "Old McDonald Had a Farm."
   Old MacDonald had a farm. Ee-i-ee-i-o.
   *And on his farm he had a **duck**. Ee-i-ee-i-o.*
   *With a **quack-quack** here,*
   *And a **quack-quack** there,*
   *Here a **quack**, there a **quack**,*
   *Everywhere a **quack-quack**.*
   Old MacDonald had a farm. Ee-i-ee-i-o.

2. Suggest that students use hand signals to identify each animal on the farm. Teach students the following sign language.

3. Repeat the verse, substituting animal names, hand signals, and sounds for the words in bold type.

 Cow: Close right hand into a fist and extend little finger and thumb only. Place thumb against side of head at temple, with little finger extending upward. Twist hand to point the little finger up and then forward several times

 Duck: Create a duckbill with index finger, middle finger, and thumb. Place it beside mouth; open and close it several times.

 Pig: Place right flat hand under chin with fingers pointing left. Bend and unbend hand several times from knuckles.

 Chick: Make a beak by putting together your index finger and thumb. Hold it over the palm of your other hand; open and close the beak.

 Horse: Create a fist with right hand. Extend index finger, middle finger, and thumb. Place thumb against right temple. Move index and middle fingers forward and back, imitating movement of horse's ears.

 Cat: Stroke an imaginary pair of whiskers on either side of your face using your thumbs and index fingers on both hands.

 Dog: Pat knee with right hand; then snap fingers.

The Long and the Short of It: Rhythm Chart

Materials

musical instrument, such as a recorder

rubber bands

chart paper

Skills Objectives

Recognize that the length of music notes can vary.

Recognize and repeat a simple rhythm.

Understand that music can be read and written.

A **Rhythm Chart** helps students see that music, like language, can be read and written. Once students can identify long and short notes, they can begin to produce both kinds of sounds and read a simple rhythm chart.

1. Discuss the terms *short* and *long* with students. Ask: *Who can tell me what* short *means? Who can tell me what* long *means? Who can show me?* Encourage students to compare the length of various items in the classroom.

2. Explain that sounds can be short or long. Using a recorder, play a series of short notes followed by a series of long notes. Ask students to listen closely. Have them hold their hands close together whenever they hear a short note and spread their arms out wide when they hear a long note.

3. Give each student a rubber band. Play a series of musical notes and ask students to make their rubber band short (by holding it loosely) whenever they hear a short note. Ask them to stretch the rubber band whenever they hear a long note.

4. Check for understanding. Play a simple tune, and have students use their rubber bands to show the lengths of the notes.

5. After students can recognize the difference in note lengths, challenge them to recreate the notes and musical patterns. Hum a simple rhythm with long and short sounds. For example, hum a "long, short, long, long, short" sound sequence. Ask students to repeat the pattern, or rhythm.

6. Discuss how students were able to reproduce this rhythm. Establish that they imitated the rhythm they heard. Ask: *Is there a way that you can play music that you haven't heard before?* Explain that musicians write notes so other people who haven't heard the music can play it.

7. Write a simple notation on chart paper using long and short lines. Hum the rhythm for students, pointing out that the long and short lines are symbols that represent long and short notes.

8. Invite students to read the chart with you. Point to each symbol and say the words *long* and *short* as students hum the corresponding rhythm. Point to the symbols from left to right as students hum the rhythm.

9. Use this process to "read" a few more rhythm sequences. Explain to students that the symbols they have read are similar to the musical notes musicians read and write. By reading and writing, musicians can play music they have never heard before.

Feel the Music: Drawing

Materials

butcher paper

instrumental music with a variety of tempos

CD or cassette player

drawing paper

crayons or markers

Skills Objective

Recognize that music has various tempos that convey different feelings.

Drawing is a useful strategy for helping students graphically represent their understanding of a concept. In this activity, students interpret music through drawing.

1. Before beginning the activity, cover worktables with butcher paper.

2. Invite students to close their eyes and listen as you play a recording of instrumental music. Have them open their eyes and talk about how the music made them feel. Discuss ways in which people share their feelings and establish that people can express their feelings through art, such as music.

3. Continue playing the music while you distribute art supplies. Encourage students to draw markings inspired by what they hear. They might use "quick marks" to reflect a staccato tempo or bold lines in response to a loud movement. They might also draw wavy or curly lines when the music is light and whimsical.

4. Encourage students to draw what they feel and be creative! Suggest that they switch colors when the music changes. Remind students to concentrate on expressing the music rather than the results of their drawing.

5. Repeat this activity over time using different musical selections. Encourage students to identify favorite pieces of music. Ask them to talk about their drawings and recall the music that inspired them.

See and Sing Your Name: Interactive Chart

Skills Objectives
See and recognize names in print.
Interact with song lyrics.

Materials

sentence strips

index cards

pocket chart

Music, rhythm, rhyme, and rap are some of the most powerful strategies you can use in helping students retain content. Song charts and oversized songbooks are essential elements in a print-rich kindergarten classroom. **Interactive Charts**, in which words can be changed, provide opportunities for students to see their names in print.

1. Print the following song lyrics on sentence strips, one line per strip. Print the name of each child on an index card, along with the pronouns *He* and *She*.

   Who is in Our Class Today?

   Tune: "Do You Know the Muffin Man?"

   Who is in our class today?

   Who will learn? Who will play?

   _____ *is in our class today.*

   _____ *will learn and play.*

2. Arrange the strips in a pocket chart. Fill in the first blank with a name card and the second blank with the corresponding pronoun card.

3. Sing the song for students. Then repeat the song, pointing to the words in the chart as you sing. Insert different name and pronoun cards in the chart. Read the new lines and sing the song again.

4. Sing the song each day, inserting a new name each time. Place the pocket chart in the classroom literacy center where students can explore and manipulate the text.

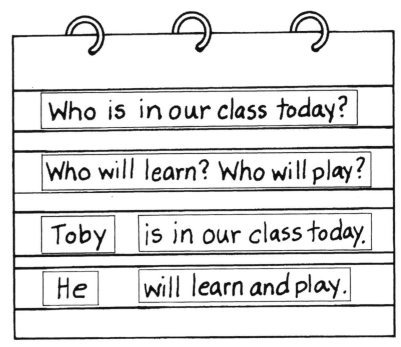

References

Bromley, K., Irwin-De Vitis, L., & Modlo, M. (1995). *Graphic organizers: Visual strategies for active learning.* New York, NY: Scholastic Professional Books.

Gardner, H. (1983). *Frames of mind: The theory of multiple intelligences.* New York, NY: Basic Books.

Hall, T., & Strangman, N. (2002). *Graphic organizers.* Retrieved August 15, 2006, from the CAST Universal Design for Learning Web site: www.cast.org/publications/ncac/ncac_go.html.

Hyerle, D. (1996). *Visual tools for constructing knowledge.* Alexandria, VA: Association for Supervision and Curriculum Development (ASCD).

Jensen, E., & Johnson, G. (1994). *The learning brain.* San Diego, CA: Turning Point for Teachers.

McCarthy, B. (1990). Using the 4MAT system to bring learning styles to schools. *Educational Leadership, 48*(2), 31–37.

National Council for the Social Studies. (2002). *Expectations of excellence: Curriculum standards for social studies.* Silver Spring, MD: National Council for the Social Studies (NCSS).

National Council of Teachers of English and International Reading Association. (1996). *Standards for the English language arts.* Urbana, IL: National Council of Teachers of English (NCTE).

National Council of Teachers of Mathematics. (2005). *Principles and standards for school mathematics.* Reston, VA: National Council of Teachers of Mathematics (NCTM).

National Research Council. (2005). *National science education standards.* Washington, DC: National Academy Press.

Nyberg, J. (1996). *Charts for children.* Glenview, IL: Good Year Books.

Ogle, D. M. (2000). Make it visual: A picture is worth a thousand words. In M. McLaughlin & M. Vogt (Eds.), *Creativity and innovation in content area teaching.* Norwood, MA: Christopher-Gordon.

Seefeldt, C. (2002). *Creating rooms of wonder.* Beltsville, MD: Gryphon House.

Tate, M. L. (2003). *Worksheets don't grow dendrites: 20 instructional strategies that engage the brain.* Thousand Oaks, CA: Corwin Press.

Printed in the United States
By Bookmasters